The Eternal Fires

Why I Believe in Hell

Valarie Owen

HYATT PRESS * 2020
Grapevine, Texas 76051

The Eternal Fires: Why I Believe in Hell
By Valarie Owen

Published by Hyatt Press
A Subsidiary of Hyatt Int'l Ministries, Incorporated

Mailing Addresses (2020)
Hyatt Int'l Ministries
Attention: Valarie Owen
P. O. Box 3877
Grapevine, TX 76099

Internet Addresses
Email: owenvalarie@yahoo.com
FaceBook: facebook.com/valarie.owen.7

Book Design and Cover: Susan Stubbs Hyatt

ISBN: 978-1-888435-50-4

Contents

Foreword 4
Preface 5

Chapter

1. Hell Is Real *8*
2. The Rich Man and Lazarus *21*
3. Why Hell Was Created *34*
4. Where Is Hell? *39*
5. Hell Is a Place of Total Darkness *46*
6. Who Goes to Hell? *62*
7. Witchcraft *77*
8. The Devil and His Angels *91*
9. Repent or Perish *108*
10. 5 Reasons I Still Believe in Hell *121*
11. How to Be Saved *134*

About the Author *136*
Other Books by Valarie Owen *138*

ঌ Foreword ঌ

Valarie Owen is a long-time, close friend and colleague in ministry. She is a woman of deep faith and is a powerful prayer warrior. For many years, when Sue and I have needed prayer support, we have called on Valarie.

Valarie's faith arises out of her love for God's Word and her knowledge of it. She is a passionate student of Scripture and anointed Bible teacher. For many years, she taught informative, inspiring, faith-building Bible courses at Word of Faith Bible College in Farmers Branch (Dallas-Fort Worth Metroplex), Texas, and at Calvary Bible College in Fort Worth, Texas. She has also ministered in churches and conferences around the world.

This, her most recent book, is written out of her love and deep concern for those who do not know Christ, as well as out of her desire to awaken sleeping Christians to the reality of hell. I believe you will be deeply stirred as you read *The Eternal Fires: Why I Believe in Hell.*

Eddie L. Hyatt, D.MIN., M.DIV., M.A.
Grapevine, Texas
May 2020

Preface

There is a face-to-face fellowship that all Christians should maintain with the Lord in their prayer time. And there is also a face-to-face encounter that every person will have with the Our Creator, the God of Universe, and the question will be asked "WHAT DID YOU DO WITH JESUS?"

The purpose of this book is not to express what I think about hell, nor is it to contend with those who have attitudes and interpretations that differ from mine. It is, instead, to explore the Scriptures and learn what Jesus taught.

I want to encourage my readers to stay with the Word of God, and not to fall prey to the traditions of men. My heartfelt desire is that you will always allow *The Teacher*—the Holy Spirit of God—*to lead you into all truth (John 16:13).* Remain obedient to the Lord. You can trust Him. Perhaps when you least expect it, He will speak to you and through you. He has done that many times for me over the years, but I remember one occasion, in particular, when He did that when I was buying a new car.

The young salesman offered me the keys to take a test drive. I asked him if he would drive and demonstrate it for me. So, he got into the car with me, and when he saw my Bible and notes on the seat, he said, "I'm an atheist."

I quickly responded, "Thirty seconds after you're dead, you won't be!" I have now had several years to think about that encounter! I remember that his wife called to thank me for what I had said to him. It seems those few words had a real impact on him because he talked to her about it. She said that normally this would not have happened because, until that evening, he had never allowed any reference to God to be mentioned in their home. She thanked me. How could I ever forget that encounter? And yes, I bought the car.

Now, if God thought it necessary for me to know the young man's outcome, He would have shown me, but He hasn't. However, I know that I can I trust His Word that tells me that it will not return void and will accomplish His purposes. So, as you are reading the words of Jesus in this book, keep in mind something that Isaiah wrote:

> [11]*So shall My word be that goes forth from My mouth; It shall not return to Me void, But it shall accomplish what I please, And it shall prosper in the thing for which I sent it (Isaiah 55:11).*

Another thing to keep in mind as you read God's Word is that it contains many word pictures and various literary devices, such as metaphors, similes, symbols, types and shadows, allegories, emblems, and parables. These are tools for communication. Hosea refers to this:

> [10]*I have also spoken by the prophets, and have multiplied visions; I have given symbols through the witness of the prophets (Hosea 12:10).*

When Jesus' Disciples asked Him why He sometimes spoke in parables, He explained the meaning of these parables to them. Today, some readers don't understand symbolic language, but to rightly divide the Word of God, it is important to know that behind every figure of speech there is a point of truth.

> [10]*And the disciples came and said to Him, "Why do You speak to them in parables?"* [11]*He answered and said to them, "Because it has been given to you to know the mysteries of the kingdom of heaven, but to them it has not been given (Matthew 13:10-11).*

In this study, we're going to see that hell is not one of those literary devices or figures of speech. It is real.

Chapter 1

Hell Is Real

And the angels who did not keep their proper domain, but left their own abode,
He has reserved
in everlasting chains under darkness
for the judgment of the great day.
Jude 6

Hell is not a fairy tale. Hell is real. If you believe in the Bible, you must believe in hell because it is mentioned throughout its pages. If you believe in Jesus, you must believe in hell because He taught about hell and warned people to make every effort not to go there. Since He is both Lord and Savior, it behooves us to listen to Him.

The Book of John holds a unique place among the records of the life of Jesus Christ, Our Lord. The Apostle John, who was called *A Son of Thunder,* shows clearly that Our Lord is *The Eternal Word* and *God Incarnate.* Jesus is the Son of the Father God and He came down as a human being to tabernacle among us. Deity walked this earth!

I can relate to the Gordon Lindsay (1906-1973) who so aptly said, "To attempt to write about the Son of God, the Man from Nazareth, one feels keenly his own inadequacy." I feel a similar sense of inadequacy in writing this book about hell, but it is something God placed on my heart many years ago, and I am thankful now for the opportunity to do it.

What Jesus Taught Is Most Important

In preparing the way for Jesus, John the Baptist preached in the wilderness of Judea, and his focus was "REPENT!"

> *Repent for the kingdom of heaven is at hand.*
> *Matthew 3:1-2*

Then, when Jesus came, sent by God to fulfill the law and to redeem lost humanity, He also proclaimed, "REPENT!"

With this in mind, we need to consider Paul's words in his letter to the Galatians, and we need to hold them close to our heart as we go through this study in God's Word.

> *4But when the fullness of the time had come, God sent forth His Son, born of a virgin, born under the law, 5to redeem those who were under the law, that we might receive the adoption as sons (Galatians 4:4-5).*

We also need to keep this in mind because, sadly, many false doctrines have crept into the Church. It seems that no matter what is taught, if it is on the radio or the television, many assume it is Gospel truth. But that's not necessarily so! A warning in Revelation comes to mind!

> *19And if anyone takes away from the words of the book of this prophecy, God shall take away his part from the Book of Life, from the holy city, and from the things which are written in this book (Revelation 22:19).*

Jesus Came to Save Us from Hell

In Matthew 4:12-25, we find the account of the beginning of Jesus' ministry in Galilee. It's good to remember that, in this passage, quite a bit of time elapsed between the events of verses 11 and 12. The events that took place during that period are covered in the Gospel of John (1:29-5:47).

Once John the Baptist was imprisoned, Jesus went to Galilee where he began proclaiming: *The Kingdom of God is at hand (Matthew 4:17).*

> [23]*And Jesus went about all Galilee, teaching in their synagogues, preaching the gospel of the kingdom, and healing all kinds of sickness and all kinds of disease among the people.* [24]*Then His fame went throughout all Syria; and they brought to Him all sick people who were afflicted with various diseases and torments, and those who were demon-possessed, epileptics, and paralytics; and He healed them.* [25]*Great multitudes followed Him from Galilee, and from Decapolis, Jerusalem, Judea, and beyond the Jordan (Matthew 4:23-25).*

Every time that I study these verses, I am reminded that many people want to question how God could condemn to hell those who have never heard the Gospel. Read the verses again—slowly. The thing to remember is that God is a faithful, loving Savior who desires that all people accept His Way of Salvation.

Matthew speaks of one occasion when the crowds following Jesus grew so large that He climbed a mountain to find a convenient place to teach His Disciples. (Matthew 4:25-5:1-2). Among the many things that He said to them was:

> *[17]Do not think that I came to destroy the Law or the Prophets. I did not come to destroy but to fulfill. [18]For assuredly, I say to you, till heaven and earth pass away, one jot or one tittle will by no means pass from the law till all is fulfilled. [19]Whoever therefore breaks one of the least of these commandments, and teaches men so, shall be called least in the kingdom of heaven; but whoever does and teaches them, he shall be called great in the kingdom of heaven. [20]For I say to you, that unless your righteousness exceeds the righteousness of the Scribes and Pharisees, you will by no means enter the Kingdom of Heaven. You have heard that it was said to those of old, 'You shall not murder, and whoever murders will be in danger of the judgment.' [22]But I say to you that whoever is angry with his brother without a cause shall be in danger of the council...But whoever says, 'You fool!' shall be in danger of hell fire (Matthew 5:17-22).*

So once again, Jesus spoke of hell.

The Blood of Jesus Is Enough!

The only way to miss hell is to accept the finished work of Calvary where Jesus shed His Blood on a wooden cross as a sacrifice for us. This is the only act in all of history that has made possible our escape from hell and that can put us on the road to heaven. The indisputable fact is that there are not several ways to get to heaven. Jesus is *THE Way*—the Only Way. Yet, during my research for this book, I discovered that several preachers teach that the sacrificial Blood of Jesus is not enough for salvation. That is false!

The First, Second, and Third Heavens and Hell

I must refute something else! The devil is not in hell. And he is not roaming around heaven. What do the Scriptures tell us? His headquarters is in what is called *the second heaven.* According to the Creation narrative in Genesis, God created the heavens—plural—and the earth. Providing further insight, Paul speaks of a man whom he knew who was caught up to *the third heaven.*

> [2]*I know a man in Christ who fourteen years ago—whether in the body I do not know, or whether out of the body I do not know, God knows—such a one was caught up to the third heaven.* [3]*And I know such a man—whether in the body or out of the body I do not know, God knows—(II Corinthians 12:2-3).*

So, it is only logical to assume that, if there is *a third heaven,* there must also be *a first heaven* and *a second heaven.*

What about Paradise?

Scripture tells us about hell. For example, before Jesus' Resurrection, hell consisted of two compartments. The first compartment is called *paradise,* and it is the dwelling place of the souls of the righteous who had died. The second compartment is the dwelling place of the souls of the unrighteous. When Jesus ascended to heaven, He took with Him the souls who were in paradise. Paradise was not in heaven until after the Resurrection.

Cleansing the Heavenly Utensils

Another—and often-overlooked accomplishment of Jesus'

Resurrection—is something that I really love: Jesus' Blood cleansed the heavenly utensils. The writer of Hebrews explains it this way:

> [21]*Then likewise he sprinkled with blood both the tabernacle and all the vessels of the ministry.* [22]*And according to the law almost all things are purified with blood, and without shedding of blood there is no remission.*
>
> [23]*Therefore it was necessary that the copies of the things in the heavens should be purified with these, but the heavenly things themselves with better sacrifices than these.* [24]*For Christ has not entered the holy places made with hands, which are copies of the true, but into heaven itself, now to appear in the presence of God for us;* [25]*not that He should offer Himself often, as the high priest enters the Most Holy Place every year with blood of another—* [26]*He then would have had to suffer often since the foundation of the world; but now, once at the end of the ages, He has appeared to put away sin by the sacrifice of Himself (Hebrews 9:21-26).*

Motives Matter as Much as Action

Whereas the *Law of Moses* dealt only with the act of sin, *The Law of Christ* deals with the motivation of a person's heart, which was the root cause of the act. In Jesus' *Sermon on the Mount (Matthew 5-7),* He raised the standard regarding guilt. For example, He did not mention the actual act of murder, which had to be punished. He spoke, instead, about the sins of the heart, teaching that they are on the same level as the overt acts of the sins themselves. So, rather than declaring how Jesus did away with the law, it is best to read this again to understand what He was really saying. He teaches that, if we come to the altar to offer the sacrifice of praise, we must first deal with all unforgiveness we might harbor. Only then can we offer acceptable praise.

Yes, Hell is Horrible!

Hell is a horrible reality. It is also a horrible place. It seems that most Christians shudder at the thought of a sermon on something so awful. Yet, it has been said that no one ever preached a more powerful message about hell than did Jesus Himself. He is the first person in the New Testament to mention it. He plainly testifies that hell is a place of fire, and as we study Scripture, we will see that hell is a real place with a specific location. From His teaching, we learn two things about hell: it has gates and it is eternal.

So, first, Jesus taught that hell has gates. He uses this term in talking to Peter: *Upon this rock I will build my Church; and the GATES OF HELL shall not prevail against it (Matthew 16:18).* Not only does Jesus acknowledge that hell cannot overcome His work, but also, that He is the One holding the keys to those gates (Revelation 1:18). Keys are the tools that represent the ability to lock and unlock an entrance, as well as the authority to do so.

Then, too, Peter recognized Jesus' divine power and authority by acknowledging that He was the Promised Messiah. He called Him *Son of God!* This was not a figment of Peter's imagination. God Himself had given Peter this revelation.

Furthermore, in this passage, Jesus was talking about laying the foundation of His Church. He was telling Peter that this revelation of His identity was, in fact, the very foundation of The Church.

So, Jesus Himself oversees the building of His Church. The Disciples were to be His original, chosen leaders with the responsibility and authority to offer salvation to the world through the proclamation of Who He is. This same task is the responsibility of every believer. This is clear in verse 19, where the Greek word translated "you" is plural, and it is confirmed in The Great Commission (Matthew 28:16-20).

So again, referring to keys, they can be used to unlock doors, but they can also be used to lock them. This thought alerts us to the authority the Lord has entrusted to us who believe in Him, and that is the authority to bind and loose.

> [16]*And I will give you the keys of the kingdom of heaven, and whatever you bind on earth will be bound in heaven, and whatever you loose on earth will be loosed in heaven" (Matthew 16:19).*

> [18]*Assuredly, I say to you, whatever you bind on earth will be bound in heaven, and whatever you loose on earth will be loosed in heaven (Matthew 18:18).*

The authority to do this binding and loosing depends on acceptance of the Gospel. But whoever might choose to reject the offer of salvation does not have this authority and will pass through the gates into hell.

Jesus is saying that we have responsibility to cooperate with God. Bible teacher, Dr. Fuchsia Pickett (d. 2004) confirmed this by noting that the true reading of this passage is that we are to bind and loose on earth what *has already loosed and bound in heaven.* This echoes something Jesus said:

> [18]*Then Jesus answered and said to them, "Most assuredly, I say to you, the Son can do nothing of Himself, but what He sees the Father do; for whatever He does, the Son also does in like manner (John 5:19).*

In Revelation, Jesus says this:

> *I am he that liveth, and was dead; and, behold, I am alive for evermore, Amen; and have the keys of hell and of death (Revelation 1:18, KJV).*

Thanks to the Father for sending Jesus to conquer death, hell, and the grave for us. Heaven's Door is open!

Unquenchable Fire

When Jesus denounced the Pharisees for false teachings, He spoke eight woes upon them, including their destiny to spend eternity in hell. His rebuke was harsh: *You serpents. You generation of vipers! How can you escape the damnation of hell? (Matthew 23:33).*

Scripture records Jesus' use of the term *hell's fire* several times. Mark records His hard-hitting message (Mark 9:43-48), using figurative language to drive home His message.

> [42]*"But whoever causes one of these little ones who believe in Me to stumble, it would be better for him if a millstone were hung around his neck, and he were thrown into the sea.* [43]*If your hand causes you to sin, cut it off. It is better for you to enter into life maimed, rather than having two hands, to go to hell, into the fire that shall never be quenched—* [44]*where 'Their worm does not die and the fire is not quenched.'*

> *[45]And if your foot causes you to sin, cut it off. It is better for you to enter life lame, rather than having two feet, to be cast into hell, into the fire that shall never be quenched—[46]where 'Their worm does not die and the fire is not quenched.' [47]And if your eye causes you to sin, pluck it out. It is better for you to enter the kingdom of God with one eye, rather than having two eyes, to be cast into hell fire—[48]where 'Their worm does not die and the fire is not quenched' (Mark 9:42-48).*

Note that the expressions *the worm does not die* and *the fire is not quenched*. In this passage, Jesus is using these to help teach the seriousness of sin and its consequences. He speaks of *hell* three times and He uses the word "fire" six times. Hell is a place of torment, a place of everlasting physical and emotional torment. This describes the horrible fate that awaits those who reject the Cross and the Blood of Jesus to save. To believe that hell is merely symbolic is a complete denial of the truth of the Holy Bible.

Punishment Awaits Transgressors

There are 66 books in the Bible, and in the Old Testament, there are 66 chapters that declare the coming of a Savior. One of these passages is in Isaiah. In it, the Prophet shows a contrast between true and false worship. He also describes the punishment awaiting those who transgress against the God of Creation. It is important to remember that God is far above humanity, and laws decided by mere mortals cannot make right what God has declared sinful. So, laws that people pass legalizing sin do not change the fact that sin is still sin in God's eyes.

[22]"For as the new heavens and the new earth which I will make shall remain before Me," says the Lord, "So shall your descendants and your name remain. [23]And it shall come to pass that from one New Moon to another, And from one Sabbath to another, all flesh shall come to worship before Me," says the Lord. [24]"And they shall go forth and look upon the corpses of the men who have transgressed against Me. For their worm does not die, and their fire is not quenched. They shall be an abhorrence to all flesh" (Isaiah 66:22-24).

Jesus' words recorded in Mark 9:48 confirm Isaiah 66:24. One version translates the passage in Mark this way: *This is where the maggots never die and the fire never goes out!* The imagery in this passage is probably based on the Valley of Hinnom, Jerusalem's garbage heap where unclean corpses were thrown and were decomposing.

Also in this passage, the word "transgressed" is a synonym for the word "rebelled." It is also helpful to know that, when Isaiah uses the image of the worm never dying, he is painting a word picture of eternal punishment. The use of *New Moons* and *Sabbaths* shows that the worship of God by His people is an action that is ongoing eternally and not merely a temporary practice.

[3]Also their slain shall be thrown out; their stench shall rise from their corpses, and the mountains shall be melted with their blood (Isaiah 34:3).

This warning extends to our day and applies to those who call themselves Christians but who knowingly practice sin.

[20]Woe to those who call evil good, and good evil; Who put darkness for light, and light for darkness; Who put bitter

for sweet, and sweet for bitter. [21]Woe to those who are wise in their own eyes, and prudent in their own sight (Isaiah 5:20-21).

We must be careful, then! We must open our hearts to accept Jesus as Savior and Lord, for hell will be overloaded with those who dismiss the truth and smirk at the reality of hell. Jesus came to make a way of escape for us by shedding His Precious Blood. It behooves us to honor that!

[25]The anger of the LORD is aroused against His people; He has stretched out His hand against them and stricken them, and the hills trembled. Their carcasses were as refuse in the midst of the streets. For all this His anger is not turned away, but His hand is stretched out still (Isaiah 5:25).

When God Gets Angry

It is clear that God is angry with His people who fall into idol worship and who question His faithfulness. In fact, the Old Testament abounds with warnings about this through His prophets. He is an awesome God! His Word says that He stretched out His Hand in anger and the hills trembled!

[18]Then the earth shook and trembled; The foundations of the hills also quaked and were shaken, Because He was angry (Psalm 18:7).

[25]Therefore the anger of the Lord is aroused against His people; He has stretched out His hand against them and stricken them, and the hills trembled. Their carcasses were as refuse in the midst of the streets. For all this His anger is not turned away, but His hand is stretched out still (Isaiah 5:25).

[4]I beheld the mountains, and indeed they trembled, and all the hills moved back and forth (Jeremiah 4:24).

This describes the awful impact suffered by the Israelites as a result of King Saul's sin and corruption. They had been warned by God though Samuel, yet they rebelled, insisting on their own way. This rebellion was against God and His Word, and rebellion is the same as witchcraft.

[23]For rebellion is as the sin of witchcraft, and stubbornness is as iniquity and idolatry. Because you have rejected the word of the Lord, He also has rejected you from being king (I Samuel 15:23).

God spoke, but His own people did not believe Him. That brought serious consequences! It still does!

Man's laws cannot make moral
what God has declared to be immoral.
Even if sin is legalized by human law,
it is still sin in the eyes of God.

Chapter 2

The Rich Man and Lazarus

> *Therefore, He says: "When He ascended on high, He led captivity captive, and gave gifts to men." Now this, "He ascended"—what does it mean but that He also first descended into the lower parts of the earth?*
>
> *Ephesians 4:8-9*

It is clear that Jesus believed in a place called *hell* and that it is a place of eternal torment. Yet, despite this and the fact that many Scriptures speak of hell, there are those who choose to ignore it or even to shrug it off. It seems that the average Christian today does not realize that Jesus came to this earth to save us from this place—a real place where God pours of His judgment. So, it is important to set the record straight, and as we do this, the Holy Spirit will guide us into all truth and open our understanding (John 16:13).

Have we Christians become dull and unaware of the sin that is running rampant in our world today? What a tragedy that so many precious souls are spending forever in hell! Do we care? Are we not moved to action by compassion, knowing that mothers are suffering as millions of babies are murdered in the womb or at birth? Do we turn aside from those who feel hopeless and are committing suicide at the rate of one person every 40 seconds? So many are slipping into hell every day, and yet we seem to turn our backs on their eternal destination—a very real hell. Has the truth of a real hell been erased so completely from our thinking?

Is it possible that, for too long, we have assumed that all is well, while all the time the fires of hell are burning? While we remain passive, preoccupied, and perhaps ignorant, Satan is busy equipping his demons with every tactic imaginable to capture the souls of men, women, and children.

This ignorance about hell was exposed in a recent interview with a punk-rocker. When she was asked about her greatest desire, she replied, "To die and go to hell." She said that she wanted to go to hell because it would be lots of fun. How wrong she was! What a tragedy! Hell is no joke. Does she represent many in a generation that has no concept of the reality of a literal, burning hell?

The horrific nature of hell is described by Luke in a story that Jesus told. It is the story of a rich man and a poor man named Lazarus.

> *There was a certain rich man who was clothed in purple*
> *and fine linen and fared sumptuously every day.* 20*But*
> *there was a certain beggar named Lazarus, full of sores,*
> *who was laid at his gate,* 21*desiring to be fed with the*
> *crumbs which fell from the rich man's table. Moreover,*
> *the dogs came and licked his sores.* 22*So it was that the*
> *beggar died and was carried by the angels to Abraham's*
> *bosom. The rich man also died and was buried.*
>
> 23*And being in torments in Hades [The KJV renders this*
> *"hell."], he lifted up his eyes and saw Abraham afar off,*

> *and Lazarus in his bosom. 24Then he cried and said,*
> *"Father Abraham, have mercy on me, and send Lazarus*
> *that he may dip the tip of his finger in water and cool my*
> *tongue; for I am tormented in this flame." 25But Abraham*
> *said, "Son, remember that in your lifetime you received*
> *your good things, and likewise Lazarus evil things; but*
> *now he is comforted and you are tormented. 26And besides*
> *all this, between us and you there is a great gulf fixed, so*
> *that those who want to pass from here to you cannot, nor*
> *can those from there pass to us."*
>
> *27Then he said, "I beg you therefore, father, that you*
> *would send him to my father's house, 28for I have five*
> *brothers, that he may testify to them, lest they also come*
> *to this place of torment." 29Abraham said to him, "They*
> *have Moses and the prophets; let them hear them." 30And*
> *he said, "No, father Abraham; but if one goes to them from*
> *the dead, they will repent." 31But he said to him, "If they do*
> *not hear Moses and the prophets, neither will they be*
> *persuaded though one rise from the dead"* (Luke 16:19-31).

This story is not a parable. Jesus gives us the report of a real situation, and in it, He compares the condition of each of the two men. On the one hand, in his earthly life, a certain rich man lacked nothing. Life was good! He had everything he needed to keep him totally comfortable. On the other hand, Lazarus was a poor man who lay at the gate of the rich man's house, begging for something to eat. Jesus' use of a real person named *Lazarus* helps us understand that He is telling a real story and that He is not simply providing a made-up illustration or telling a parable. By the way, the name *Lazarus* means "God, My Help."

In another story—one recorded by John—a different Lazarus takes center stage (John 11:1-27). He is the Lazarus whom Jesus raised from the dead. In this story, John writes that there was *a certain man* by the name of Lazarus of Bethany who was sick. So, when Luke relates the story that Jesus told about *a certain man* and Lazarus (Luke 16:19-31), he is not referring to the Lazarus of Bethany, but the second person in the narrative is *a certain rich man.* I believe these writings by Luke and John confirm that these are real people. Some scholars have speculated that the rich man's personal name was *Dives,* as the Latin Vulgate suggests.

Eternal Is Forever

By the Scriptures, we have established the fact that a real hell exists. This hell is everlasting and eternal. The Greek word that describes this idea is the adjective *aiōnion.* This word is used to describe both eternal bliss and eternal punishment. It is used by Matthew in describing Jesus' description of hell: *"Then He will also say to those on the left hand, 'Depart from Me, you cursed, into the everlasting [aiōnion] fire prepared for the devil and his angels'" (Matthew 25:41).*

If we really believe in the inerrancy of the Bible, we must acknowledge the existence of hell, a reality taught by Jesus Himself. As Gordon Lindsey (1906-1973) rightly noted, hell is a difficult subject with which to deal, but it is a Biblical reality with which we must grapple.

Two Popular Heresies

Regarding teaching about our eternal destiny, two popular heresies are currently making the rounds, and they have even infiltrated churches that would consider themselves to be Spirit-filled and Bible-believing. The first heresy teaches that we will be afforded a second chance to determine our eternal destiny after we die. The second heresy teaches that Jesus' death on the Cross was not sufficient for our salvation. It teaches, instead, that He had to go to hell and to suffer spiritually to provide for our salvation. Neither of these doctrines has any basis in Scripture. They are pure heresy.

In the case of Jesus' story about the rich man, there is no indication that he was given a second chance to seek forgiveness. He knew that his personal destiny was firmly fixed, but he did express concern for those who were still alive (Luke 16:19-31).

No doubt, one heresy is as cruel as another, but perhaps the most serious of all is to deny the efficacy of the shed Blood of Jesus. That denial will surely send the unrepentant person to the pit.

Only One Gospel

Paul, in his letter to the Galatians, expresses amazement and deep concern about how quickly the new believers had turned away from the Jesus he had preached and the true Gospel. Obviously, these people had fallen prey to false teachers and their seductive, heretical ideas. Paul writes:

> [6]*I marvel that you are turning away so soon from Him who called you in the grace of Christ, to a different gospel,*
> [7]*which is not another; but there are some who trouble you and want to pervert the gospel of Christ.* [8]*But even if we, or an angel from heaven, preach any other gospel to you than what we have preached to you, let him be accursed.*

> [9]*As we have said before, so now I say again, if anyone preaches any other gospel to you than what you have received, let him be accursed.*[10]*For do I now persuade men, or God? Or do I seek to please men? For if I still pleased men, I would not be a bondservant of Christ (Galatians 1:6-10).*

There is only one God, and we are to serve only Him. Jesus made this clear in Luke 16:1-18 through His parable of the unjust steward. The point of the story is that no one can serve two masters. We cannot serve God and mammon (Matthew 6:24). *Mammon* refers to greed, money, wealth, and treasure. When the Pharisees, who were lovers of mammon, ridiculed Jesus, He rebuked them sharply:

> *You* are *those who justify yourselves before men, but God knows your hearts. For what is highly esteemed among men is an abomination in the sight of God (Luke 16:15).*

Abraham's Bosom

In his earthly life, the beggar in the story of The Rich Man and Lazarus seemed only to want to be allowed to eat the crumbs that fell from the rich man's table. But when he died, the angels carried him to a place of honor in the abode of the righteous dead, a place called *Abraham's Bosom (Luke 16:22)*. One thing that this story teaches us is that our status in eternity may differ greatly from whatever it might have been during our life on earth.

The reference to Abraham's Bosom is significant because it points to the blessing on Abraham, a blessing that God had imparted by means of the Blood Covenant that He had made with Abraham (Genesis 12:1-4).

1Now the Lord had said to Abram:
"Get out of your country, from your family and from your
father's house, to a land that I will show you. 2I will make
you a great nation; I will bless you and make your name
great; and you shall be a blessing. 3I will bless those who
bless you, and I will curse him who curses you; and in you
all the families of the earth shall be blessed." 4So Abram
departed as the Lord had spoken to him, and Lot went with
him. And Abram was seventy-five years old when he
departed from Haran (Genesis 12:1-4).

Another significant point made in this story is that when the rich man died and his body was buried, his soul was in torment in Hades [hell]. It was from this place that he saw Abraham across the gulf that separated Paradise from hell (Luke 16:26).

Paradise is the place that Jesus visited in spirit while His body lay in the tomb. All of the Patriarchs on the Paradise side of Hades were excited to see Him. They were experiencing the fulfillment of their prophecies that they had been waiting patiently to see (I Peter 3:18-20; Ephesians 4:9-10).

18For Christ also suffered once for sins, the just for the
unjust, that He might bring us to God, being put to death
in the flesh but made alive by the Spirit, 19by whom also
He went and preached to the spirits in prison, 20who
formerly were disobedient, when once the Divine
longsuffering waited in the days of Noah, while the ark
was being prepared, in which a few, that is, eight souls,
were saved through water (I Peter 3:18-20).

9Now this, "He ascended"—what does it mean but that

> *He also first descended into the lower parts of the earth? [10]He who descended is also the One who ascended far above all the heavens, that He might fill all things. (Ephesians 4:9-10).*

At this time, the physical bodies of the Patriarchs and the physical body of Jesus were still in the graves. But Jesus was at work in Paradise! Seeing Jesus, Moses must have exclaimed, "I told you!" And others—such as Daniel, Jeremiah, Jacob—must have been excited beyond words!

No Second Chances

Have you ever wondered where the souls of the saints of old were resting until that moment? Matthew and Mark's Gospels tell us that their bodies were still in the grave, but Luke's Gospel provides additional information through the story of *The Rich Man and Lazarus.*

The rich man is in the flames and he is crying across the chasm: *"Father Abraham, have mercy on me, and send Lazarus that he may dip the tip of his finger in water and cool my tongue; for I am tormented in this flame" (Luke 16:24).*

How long would that drop of water last in comparison to what would be needed to offer even the possibility of the slightest bit of relief throughout eternity?

This story shows other important things. For example, it shows us that those in eternity can hear, see, feel pain, and they can hear the wailing of the helpless and hopeless ones. Then, too, it shows that it was Abraham who revealed that, at that time, there was a gulf between Paradise and hell over which no one could pass. Also, the story shows how different our existence in eternity can be from life on earth, for Abraham reminds the rich man that his earthly life had been one characterized by comfort and luxury, while Lazarus had known only pain, sickness, and lack. But in eternity, how different it was!

The unrepentant will face judgement and that is not to be taken lightly! Their punishment will be according to their crimes on earth, and it will be based on the severity of those acts. But those who are saved through the one and only means of salvation, Jesus Christ, will not face this judgement. The harsh reality is that once a person dies, the scene is set. No one gets a second chance!

In the story, something interesting happens. The rich man becomes the beggar in the sense that he pleads with Abraham to send Lazarus to his five brothers to witness to them in hopes that they will escape the fires of hell. But Abraham refuses, saying that those who were still alive on earth had all they needed to know if they would simply heed the writings of Moses and the Prophets (v. 29).

But that does not settle it for the rich man! He insists that if someone would just go to them from the dead to warn them, they would repent.

Humanity has not changed. Nor has the answer! People still need a Savior. And Jesus is that Savior. He is still The Answer. The Word of God has always provided the solution for humanity's dilemma. Yet, those who will not heed the Word of God will continue to believe that hell is just a fable, and they will, to their surprise and horror, find themselves in that place of torment forever.

In the case of the rich man, it was not his wealth that was the problem. Instead, it was what he did with his wealth that was the issue. It seems that he pampered himself while ignoring the beggar. What a sad story! What horrible, eternal consequences!

Jesus Preaches in Abraham's Bosom

During the period when Jesus' body was in the grave, He was preaching to the spirits of the obedient who were in Paradise waiting for His appearing (I Peter 3:18-20). Paul mentions these spirits in Ephesians 4:8, referring to them as *captives: When He ascended on high, He led captivity captive...).* These were not captives of Satan. They were in what could be called "a holding place" until the fullness of time for their release would arrive through Jesus. The Holy Spirit began to unravel this truth to me when I was teaching the Old Testament *via* satellite in the early 1980s. I began to think about how excited those spirits in Paradise must have been when Jesus appeared and announced He was there to take them up to heaven with Him.

This is proof that the soul and spirit of a person never die. The body in the grave is dead, but the spirit and soul are very much alive. I like what Dr. Kenneth Hagin said about this whole event: "At the Resurrection, Jesus went by and got His body." Jesus, in spirit, had descended to deliver the saints of old who had died in faith. While His body lay motionless in the grave, His Spirit was active in hell on the Paradise side. John writes about this in His Gospel.

> 38*After this, Joseph of Arimathea, being a disciple of Jesus, but secretly, for fear of the Jews, asked Pilate that he might*

take away the body of Jesus; and Pilate gave him permission. So, he came and took the body of Jesus. [39]*And Nicodemus, who at first came to Jesus by night, also came, bringing a mixture of myrrh and aloes, about a hundred pounds.* [40]*Then they took the body of Jesus, and bound it in strips of linen with the spices, as the custom of the Jews is to bury.* [41]*Now in the place where He was crucified there was a garden, and in the garden a new tomb in which no one had yet been laid.* [42]*So there they laid Jesus, because of the Jews' Preparation Day, for the tomb was nearby (John 19:38-42).*

The Significance of the Handkerchief

On Resurrection morning, when Peter and John heard that Jesus' tomb was empty, they ran to see for themselves. John reached the tomb first.

> [5]*And he, stooping down and looking in, saw the linen cloths lying there; yet he did not go in.* [6]*Then Simon Peter came, following him, and went into the tomb; and he saw the linen cloths lying there,* [7]*and the handkerchief that had been around His head, not lying with the linen cloths, but folded together in a place by itself (John 20:5-7).*

Peter saw the linen cloth and the handkerchief that had been wrapped around Jesus' head. Both cloths mattered, but the folded cloth really caught his attention. In fact, it seems to have had the greatest impact on him. When he saw the folded napkin, he believed (John 20:8).

How many times had I read this passage, and yet, I had not asked the Holy Spirit why so much emphasis was put on the handkerchief?

But Jesus knew that His disciples would understand what had happened in that tomb when they saw the folded napkin!

The mystery of the folded napkin is solved when we know and understand a specific custom of the day. The table setting for a dinner guest would include a large square of linen—a napkin—placed beside the plate. If all went well, the guest would casually wrinkle the napkin and leave it near the plate. But if the guest happened to be displeased, he would either roll it up or fold it into the shape it had been at the outset of the meal and lay it to one side. This signaled the host that the guest was dissatisfied and felt neglected. It also indicated that he would not visit again! Do you get the picture?

Cultural habits of this sort are not unusual. We see an example in the old *Ben Hur* movie. When the actor is the dinner guest of the the owner of the Arabian horses, the host burps loudly at the conclusion of the meal. He then looks to his guest for the same expression. His guest gets the message and burps also, and this indicates his approval of the meal.

Utterances from The Cross

Jesus made seven statements as He hung on the Cross, dying for us. Each one is significant and deserves our full attention.

1. *Father, forgive them for they don't know what they are doing (Luke 23:24).*
2. *Today you shall be with Me in paradise (Luke 23:43).*
3. *Behold your son; behold your mother (John 19:26-27).*

4. *My God, my God, why have You forsaken Me? (Matthew 27:46).*
5. *I am thirsty (John 19:28).*
6. *It is finished! (John 19:30).*
7. *Father, into your hands I commit my spirit (Luke 23:46).*

Jesus made the second statement to the repentant thief who was also crucified that day. He said, *Today you shall be with Me in paradise*. Today. Jesus said *TODAY* this will be so. He did not put this off to some future date.

It is finished! This sixth statement has prompted a lot of discussion and debate. But while I was reading Jesus' prayer in John 17, the Holy Spirit quickened to my heart that Jesus had already settled the issue. It was already finished. He said, *I have glorified You on the earth. I have finished the work which You have given Me to do (John 17:4).*

Here is one final thought. It has to do with Jesus' fifth statement on the Cross: *I thirst*. The loss of blood in a crucifixion results in a thirst that is beyond description. That would be the cause of His crying out for a drink.

Chapter 3

Why Hell Was Created

Charles G. Finney considered hell to be
God's eternal prison house
where incorrigible rebels against God
and his kingdom will be confined and
not allowed to spoil the eternal bliss and
happiness of those who have accepted the
free mercy and grace
God has shown to us in Jesus Christ.

The Scriptures do not disclose *when* hell was created, but they do tell us *why*. Concerning the judgement at the end of the age, Matthew records what Jesus said:

> *Then the King will turn to those on the left and say, "Away with you, you cursed ones, into the eternal fire prepared for the devil and his angels" (Matthew 25:41).*

So, Jesus clearly taught about an everlasting hell, and He did so with an urgency that we tend to overlook in our casual reading of The Word. He came into this fallen world to redeem us from this hell.

Jude, who may have been a half-brother of Jesus, also wrote about the devil and his cohorts. In his epistle, he says:

> *And I remind you of the angels who did not stay within the limits of authority God gave them, but left the place*

where they belonged. God has kept them securely chained in prisons of darkness, waiting for the great day of judgment (Jude 6 NLT).

Isaiah tells us that *sheol* or *hell* has enlarged itself.

Therefore hell hath enlarged herself, and opened her mouth without measure: and their glory, and their multitude, and their pomp, and he that rejoiceth, shall descend into it (Isaiah 5:14, KJV).

When I began teaching the Old Testament, I found myself spending more and more hours in research, study, and prayer. I was moved to ask the Lord a question: "Lord, how far did man fall?" So gently He answered: "Daughter, you will never know until you start that long climb back."

Pride Goes Before a Fall

In Ezekiel 28:11-19, the Old Testament Prophet describes the fall of Satan from his exalted position in heaven. He begins by describing the fall of the King of Tyre, but then it is obvious that he moves from the natural to the spiritual and describes the fall of the spiritual being we know as Satan and the devil.

11Moreover the word of the LORD came to me, saying,
12"Son of man, take up a lamentation for the king of Tyre, and say to him, 'Thus says the Lord GOD: You were the seal of perfection, Full of wisdom and perfect in beauty.
13You were in Eden, the garden of God; Every precious stone was your covering: The sardius, topaz, and diamond, beryl, onyx, and jasper, sapphire, turquoise, and emerald with gold. The workmanship of your timbrels and pipes

was prepared for you on the day you were created. [14]"You were the anointed cherub who covers; I established you; You were on the holy mountain of God; You walked back and forth in the midst of fiery stones. [15]You were perfect in your ways from the day you were created, Till iniquity was found in you (Ezekiel 28:11-15).

Because this description includes references to musical instruments, including *timbrels and pipes,* some think that Satan was the leader of worship in heaven. Whether or not that was the case, the fact remains that iniquity was found in him, and that iniquity was pride. His heart was full of pride because of his God-given beauty, his elevated status, and his apparent wisdom. Despite all that God had given him, he became corrupt. He lost his prestige, position, and title and became the Devil, the Deceiver. As God's enemy, he is doomed to eternal, spiritual darkness in the lake of fire and brimstone. According to Revelation,

The devil, who deceived them, was cast into the lake of fire and brimstone where the beast and the false prophet are. And they will be tormented day and night forever and ever (Revelation 20:10).

Their torment in hell
goes on both day and night!
There is no relief. There is no vacation time
from it if one chooses hell
for his or her eternal abode.

The Fall of Lucifer

Pride goes before destruction,
and a haughty spirit before a fall
(Proverbs 16:18).

Pride is the common trait found in Satan, described by both Ezekiel and Isaiah in their accounts of his fall. In Isaiah's description, he is referred to as *Lucifer.*

> [12]*How you are fallen from heaven, O Lucifer, son of the morning! How you are cut down to the ground, you who weakened the nations!* [13]*For you have said in your heart: "I will ascend into heaven, I will exalt my throne above the stars of God; I will also sit on the mount of the congregation on the farthest sides of the north;* [14]*I will ascend above the heights of the clouds, I will be like the Most High."* [15]*Yet you shall be brought down to Sheol, To the lowest depths of the Pit (Isaiah 14:12-15).*

Lucifer himself chose the path that brought about his fall. God has never made a robot. In the same way, we are not robotic creations, but instead, we are created with free will and the ability to make our own choices.

Surely, we are moved to ask, "How could Lucifer risk it all and go his own way?" Yet, in the same way, millions of people are making this choice every moment of every day. The answer is found in a sin called *pride,* and pride is rebellion against Our Creator.

As a result of his fall, Lucifer abides in spiritual darkness, consigned by God to the lowest pit of hell. This verdict is pronounced in verse 15: *Yet you shall be brought down to Sheol, to the lowest depths of the Pit*. This reveals an important aspect of the love of God, and that is the severity with which He deals with sin.

Lucifer once had access to the Throne and Presence of God, but he was brought down by his own pride. Out of that pride, he boasted! Notice his 5 "I Wills" (Isaiah 14:13-14).

1. *I will ascend into heaven (vs. 13).*
2. *I will exalt my throne above the stars of God (vs. 13).*
3. *I will sit on the mount of the congregation (vs. 13).*
4. *I will ascend above the heights of the clouds (vs. 14).*
5. *I will be like the Highest (vs. 14).*

So, Lucifer is doomed to eternal spiritual darkness in the lake of fire and brimstone. This Great Deceiver tries to keep his identity and tactics hidden in order to trap, defraud, and bring damnation to as many souls as possible. And Peter warns us that the devil is like a roaring lion, and he goes about seeking victims to destroy (I Peter 5:8).

The Scriptures establish the fact that eternity is real and consists of *eternal* hell and *eternal* bliss. We get to choose which eternal destiny will be ours.

The Scriptures establish the fact
that eternity is real and consists of
eternal hell and *eternal* bliss.
We get to choose
which eternal destiny will be ours.

Chapter 4

Where Is Hell?

> *I know that whatever God does,*
> *It shall be forever.*
> *Nothing can be added to it,*
> *And nothing taken from it.*
> *God does it,*
> *that men should fear before Him.*
>
> *Ecclesiastes 3:14*

Hell is the place described in the Bible as *a bottomless pit* (Revelation 9:1,2,11; 11:7; 17:8; 20:1,3). That has always brought up a horrifying picture in my mind of people falling—with no end to that falling!

Hell is also described as a place of eternal fire accompanied by the stench of burning sulfur.

Several words are used in Scripture to refer to hell. For example, the Hebrew word *sheol* is found 65 times in the Old Testament. It is translated as "hell" 31 times; as "grave" 31 times; and as "pit" 3 times.

In the New Testament, the Greek word *hades* is translated "the pit" 3 times; "the grave" 31 times; and "hell" 31 times. Two other words are also translated "hell" in the New Testament: *tartarus* and *gehenna.*

The Old Testament *sheol* and the New Testament *hades* have the same meaning. It is the place where the unbeliever's spirit and soul will go at death, and they remain there until the resurrection of their body.

Avoid False Teachers

Jude wrote one of the most severe warnings to the saints of his day, and this admonition remains in force for us today. He exhorts believers to keep the faith and to be alert for false teachers. He acknowledges that God delivered His people from Egypt, but he also notes that God later destroyed the ones among them who did not believe, including the angels who left to follow Satan. According to Jude, they are held in everlasting chains in darkness, awaiting the day of judgment.

> [6]*And the angels which kept not their first estate, but left their own habitation, he hath reserved in everlasting chains under darkness unto the judgment of the great day.* [7]*As Sodom and Gomorrah, and the cities around them in a similar manner to these, having given themselves over to sexual immorality and going after strange flesh, are set forth as an example, suffering the vengeance of eternal fire.* [8]*Likewise also these dreamers defile the flesh, reject authority, and speak evil of dignitaries...* [11]*Woe to them! For they have gone in the way of Cain, have run greedily in the error of Balaam for profit, and perished in the rebellion of Korah (Jude 6-8, 11).*

Jude urges believers *to contend for the faith.*

> *Beloved, while I was very diligent to write to you concerning our common salvation, I found it necessary to*

write to you exhorting you to contend earnestly for the faith which was once for all delivered to the saints (Jude 3).

He cites Cain, Balaam, and Korah as examples of those who did not contend for the faith *(vs. 11).*

1. *Woe to Cain who killed his brother.*
2. *Woe to Balaam who was greedy for gain.*
3. *Woe to Korah who rebelled against Moses and Aaron.*

Numbers 16:4-14 describes the rebellion of Korah and 250 men against Moses and Aaron, and the consequences of that sin. Korah gave three grounds for the rebellion:

1. *Is it a small thing that you have not brought us up out of a land flowing with milk and honey, to kill us in the wilderness, that you should keep acting like a prince over us? (Numbers 16:13).*
2. *Moreover, you have not brought us into a land flowing with milk and honey (Numbers 16:14).*
3. *Nor given us our inheritance of fields and vineyards. Will you put out the eyes of these men? We will not come up! (Numbers 16:14).*

This rebellion in the wilderness provides significant insight and instruction.

> [4]*So when Moses heard it, he fell on his face;* [5]*and he spoke to Korah and all his company, saying, tomorrow morning the* L*ORD will show who is His and who is holy, and will cause him to come near to Him. That one whom He chooses He will cause to come near to Him.* [6]*Do this: Take censers, Korah and all your company;* [7]*put fire in them and put incense in them before the* L*ORD tomorrow, and*

> *it shall be that the man whom the LORD chooses is the holy one. You take too much upon yourselves, you sons of Levi. [8]Then Moses said to Korah, "Hear now, you sons of Levi: [9]Is it a small thing to you that the God of Israel has separated you from the congregation of Israel, to bring you near to Himself, to do the work of the tabernacle of the LORD, and to stand before the congregation to serve them; [10]and that He has brought you near to Himself, you and all your brethren, the sons of Levi, with you? And are you seeking the priesthood also? [11]Therefore you and all your company are gathered together against the LORD. And what is Aaron that you complain against him?" [12]And Moses sent to call Dathan and Abiram the sons of Eliab, but they said, "We will not come up! [13]Is it a small thing that you have brought us up out of a land flowing with milk and honey, to kill us in the wilderness, that you should keep acting like a prince over us? [14]Moreover you have not brought us into a land flowing with milk and honey, nor given us inheritance of fields and vineyards. Will you put out the eyes of these men? We will not come up!" (Numbers 16:4-14).*

When Moses heard their rebellious challenge, he *fell on his face,* a gesture showing both his humility before the Lord and his total dependence on Him. Moses then declared that God would confirm the call on his life, reminding the people that he had not acted of his own accord.

> *[28]And Moses said: "By this you shall know that the LORD has sent me to do all these works, for I have not done them of my own will. [29]If these men die naturally like all men, or if they are visited by the common fate of all men, then the LORD has not sent me. [30]But if the LORD creates a new*

thing, and the earth opens its mouth and swallows them up with all that belongs to them, and they go down alive into the pit, then you will understand that these men have rejected the LORD. [31]Now it came to pass, as he finished speaking all these words, that the ground split apart under them, [32]and the earth opened its mouth and swallowed them up, with their households and all the men with Korah, with all their goods. [33]So they and all those with them went down alive into the pit; the earth closed over them, and they perished from among the assembly (Numbers 16:28-33).

Dathan and Abiram were partners with Korah in his rebellion against Moses. Their fate? The earth opened up and swallowed them! This was a warning to others who might be predisposed to follow Korah. It is also a warning to any today who might be of the same mind!

This incident is referred to in Deuteronomy.

[6]And [remember] what He did to Dathan and Abiram the sons of Eliab, the son of Reuben: how the earth opened its mouth and swallowed them up, their households, their tents, and all the substance that was in their possession, in the midst of all Israel (Deuteronomy 11:6).

It is also referred to in Psalms.

[16]They envied Moses also in the camp, and Aaron the saint of the Lord. [17]The earth opened and swallowed up Dathan and covered the company of Abiram. [18]And a fire was kindled in their company; the flame burned up the wicked (Psalm 106:16-18, KJV).

Hell and the Story of Jonah

Matthew 12:38-40 suggests that hell is located in the heart of the earth. This passage is the record of Jesus' reply to the scribes and the Pharisees when they asked the Lord for a sign. He responded that an evil and adulterous generation demands a sign before they will believe. He went on say that no sign would be given except the sign of Jonah the prophet.

> *For as Jonah was three days and three nights in the belly of a fish, so shall the son of Man be three days and three nights in the heart of the earth (Matthew 12:40).*

This indicates where the spirit and soul of Jesus had gone as His body lay in the grave.

Degrees of Punishment in Hell

Hell is a place of judgment and punishment of the unsaved. The severity of the punishment is based on the seriousness of the sins of each person. Jesus sheds some light on this.

> [20]*Then He began to rebuke the cities in which most of His*
> *mighty works had been done, because they did not repent:*
> [21]*Woe to you, Chorazin! Woe to you, Bethsaida! For if the*
> *mighty works which were done in you had been done in*
> *Tyre and Sidon, they would have repented long ago in*
> *sackcloth and ashes.* [22]*But I say to you, it will be more*
> *tolerable for Tyre and Sidon in the day of judgment than*
> *for you.* [23]*And you, Capernaum, who are exalted to*
> *heaven, will be brought down to Hades; for if the mighty*
> *works which were done in you had been done in Sodom,*
> *it would have remained until this day.* [24]*But I say to you*

that it shall be more tolerable for the land of Sodom in the day of judgment than for you (Matthew 11:20-24).

In the Book of Revelation, John reports the same event when he describes the Great White Throne Judgement.

12*And I saw the dead, small and great, standing before God, and books were opened. And another book was opened, which is the Book of Life. And the dead were judged according to their works, by the things which were written in the books (Revelation 20:12).*

This is not the case for those who have put their faith in Jesus as Lord and Savior. We Christians were judged at Calvary, so when we stand before the Lord, it is to receive rewards, not punishment. Some wrongly teach that we will stand before the Lord and be questioned about our sins on earth. That is not Biblical! When Jesus forgives us, He never again brings up our sin.

Chapter 5

Hell Is a Place of Total Darkness

> *Sheol [hell] is naked before Him,*
> *and destruction has no covering.*
> *Job 26:6.*

Job described hell as a vast area filled with darkness where the only light is more darkness. We can hardly visualize such a place! According to Job, the realm of the dead is visible to God and the destruction of the lost is clearly seen by Him.

According to Revelation, the unsaved will be judged at the Great White Throne Judgment (Revelation 20:12) but *born again* believers will not suffer such a fate, having already been judged at Calvary. Only through the Shed Blood of Jesus have you and I escaped such judgement and received the wonderful blessing God has provided.

Since the fall of humanity (Genesis 3), a war between *the kingdom of darkness* and *the kingdom of light* has been raging for the souls of every man, woman, and child. The darkness of *the kingdom of darkness* is described by Job: [21] *[as a] land of darkness and the shadow of death,* [22]*A land as dark as darkness itself, as the shadow of death, without any order, where even the light is like darkness (Job 10:21-22).*

The Significance of the Plague of Darkness on the Egyptians

The Egyptians worshipped the sun god whom they called *Ra,* and Pharaoh was called *The Child of the Sun.* So, it is interesting that the plagues sent by God through Moses and Aaron shut down the light of the sun, creating darkness throughout the land whose inhabitants worshipped the sun. The Egyptians got the message! They understood the meaning of this darkness. It was a judgement against *Ra* and it showed that the God of the Israelites was superior to their god.

The eighth plague—the plague of locusts—also demonstrated this. This plague was so severe that the swarms of locusts blotted out the rays of the sun, leaving the land in total darkness. Locusts covered the entire land, and what the hail and fire had not destroyed, the locusts did. Nothing was left. Not a tree. Not a green plant. Nothing! But in Goshen, where the Children of Israel lived, all was well because they were protected by the Mighty Hand of God.

The ninth plague was a plague of intense darkness. The plague fell, unannounced, like a blanket of impenetrable darkness across the land. Yet, there was light in the homes of the Hebrews!

> [21]*Then the LORD said to Moses, "Stretch out your hand toward heaven, that there may be darkness over the land of Egypt, darkness which may even be felt."* [22]*So Moses stretched out his hand toward heaven, and there was thick darkness in all the land of Egypt three days.* [23]*They did not see one another; nor did anyone rise from his place for three days. But all the children of Israel had light in their dwellings (Exodus 10:21-23).*

Pharaoh was faced with a decision. Would he serve Jehovah (The God of Israel) or Satan?

What an event! He and his people were experiencing pure darkness. Darkness with not so much as a glimmer of light! Darkness so intense that it could be felt! This describes, not only what the Egyptians were feeling, but it also helps to describe hell—which is far worse! Who can find the words to describe it? It is darkness forever.

My Out-of-Body Experience

Years ago, I had an out-of-body experience. I had gone to bed, and suddenly, I found myself in a murky place that some have called *the second heaven*. I felt as if I was suspended. I was not afraid, and I immediately said, "God, either take me up or put me down." Down I went! And as I entered my body, I felt a jolt.

Increased Awareness of the Spiritual Realm

As we grow in our knowledge of the Bible, we become increasingly aware of the spiritual realm. In the process, we come to understand that the devil has assigned demons to attack, harass, and deceive in an effort to control us. And we realize that his goal is to destroy us, if he can.

Jesus Used the Expression, "Outer Darkness"

Jesus used the phrase *outer darkness* in *The Parable of the Wedding Feast* in Matthew 22. The first part of the story describes the preparation for the ceremony. This includes the sending of invitations and it explains the punishment assigned to those who refuse to accept the invitation.

> *1And Jesus answered and spoke to them again by parables and said: 2"The kingdom of heaven is like a certain king who arranged a marriage for his son, 3and sent out his servants to call those who were invited to the wedding; and they were not willing to come. 4Again, he sent out other servants, saying, "Tell those who are invited, 'See, I have prepared my dinner; my oxen and fatted cattle are killed, and all things are ready. Come to the wedding.'" 5But they made light of it and went their ways, one to his own farm, another to his business. 6And the rest seized his servants, treated them spitefully, and killed them. 7But when the king heard about it, he was furious. And he sent out his armies, destroyed those murderers, and burned up their city. 8Then he said to his servants, "The wedding is ready, but those who were invited were not worthy. 9Therefore go into the highways, and as many as you find, invite to the wedding." 10So those servants went out into the highways and gathered together all whom they found, both bad and good. And the wedding hall was filled with guests (Matthew 22:1-10).*

In a latter part of the parable, Jesus describes what happens when an individual shows up not wearing the mandatory wedding garment. The host asks the man how he happens to be there without a wedding garment. The man has no words! No defense! At this point in the story, the man is cast into outer darkness.

> *13Then the king said to the servants, "Bind him hand and foot, take him away, and cast him into outer darkness;*

there will be weeping and gnashing of teeth. [14]*For many are called, but few are chosen"* (*Matthew 22:13-14*).

Regarding the statement, *many are called but few are chosen,* Dr. Fuchsia Pickett said that this should read, "Many choose not to be chosen."

My Experiences with Total Darkness

Many years ago, I had Lasik surgery on my eyes. Something went wrong, and two days after the procedure, I was totally blind. I experienced darkness! I am sharing this because, on a previous occasion, when I had asked the Lord what hell was like, for just a few seconds, He showed me what I would describe as *total darkness.*

Once again, during this medical emergency, I experienced *total darkness.* I could not even see the light coming through the blinds. I could not see my grandchildren, nor the food the girls were setting before me. At one point, as I sat at the table to eat, one of my daughters began to help me. She explained that the meat was at "twelve o'clock." I told her not to go on. I was not hungry. I went back to my room. I knew the family was crushed and that they were praying for me.

I returned to Tylock Lasik Surgery—where it had all begun—for a checkup. When the nurse called my name and I stood up to follow her, I ran into a wall. She was not aware that I was blind!

The time had come for me to have a talk with Jesus. I don't remember all of that conversation, but I do remember telling the Lord that I would never accept this darkness. I normally don't talk about that darkness because my heart is tender about the situation and the healing I received. But I do want to say that the darkness I experienced was different from the darkness we experience when we close our eyes. It brings to mind the blindness experienced by those who are lost. They are in the dark now, but they face ultimate, eternal darkness when they die. Often, I sense the Holy Spirit weeping through me for the lost.

If you do not know Jesus as your Blood Sacrifice, please, listen to me now! That eternal darkness cannot be described. Job probably expressed it best when he said that *the only light is more darkness (Job 10:20-22).*

During my season of blindness, I continued to pray and to praise God every day, and the Holy Spirit increased my faith that I would be healed. Three days later, I saw my first glimmer of light. The first thing that I saw was my three-year-old granddaughter who had come into the room with a boom box playing loud music. What a blessing!

At no time during this awful experience did I know fear. I did have an interesting thing happen, however. And I want to give a big piece of advice right here! Someone associated with a television ministry sent a person to me, advising me to sue: "Turn this over to Mr. ___ [a lawyer], and he will make you rich." The Holy Spirit whispered "No," and that was the end of it.

Perhaps the words of the poet Robert Frost describe my Spirit-led decision: *two roads diverged, and I took the one less traveled.* The encounter with this envoy also reminded me of Jude's description of the ungodly and their fate.

[8]Likewise also these dreamers defile the flesh, reject authority, and speak evil of dignitaries. [9]Yet Michael the archangel, in contending with the devil, when he disputed about the body of Moses, dared not bring against him a reviling accusation, but said, "The Lord rebuke you!" [10]But these speak evil of whatever they do not know; and whatever they know naturally, like brute beasts, in these things they corrupt themselves. [11]Woe to them! For they have gone in the way of Cain, have run greedily in the error of Balaam for profit, and perished in the rebellion of Korah. [12]These are spots in your love feasts, while they feast with you without fear, serving only themselves. They are clouds without water, carried [h]about by the winds; late autumn trees without fruit, twice dead, pulled up by the roots; [13]raging waves of the sea, foaming up their own shame; wandering stars for whom is reserved the blackness of darkness forever (Jude 8-13).

Today Is the Day of Salvation

Dear Reader, if you fail to accept Jesus while you are alive, it will be too late once you take your final breath. You will have allowed Satan to claim another trophy—YOU!

How is it that multitudes can be so easily lured by Satan, deceived and blind to their need for Jesus, the only means of salvation? This deception commonly happens through the many false religions that abound, and none of them provide the means of paying the penalty of sin. But Christianity does. The Bible takes sin seriously. God takes sin so seriously that He mandates the penalty of eternal death for it. Only the Shed Blood of Jesus meets the requirements for deliverance from that penalty and makes salvation and eternal life possible. So, then, it is the shed Blood of Jesus that distinguishes Christianity and that differentiates it from all of the world's religions.

Those ensnared in the trap of false religions have become followers of those who believed they had found a way around the Blood Sacrifice of the Lord Jesus. To them the Cross is foolishness.

We are saved from darkness by our confession of Jesus as Lord of our life. He lives in us by His Word and Holy Spirit because we are born-again, Blood-bought children of God.

I want to say again that there are no second chances. Once a person draws their last breath and departs this life, that's it! But until then, each one of us has a choice as to where we will spend eternity.

When I taught school, we had a study hall period each day. On one occasion, a young student was sitting next to my desk and I felt to witness to him. He told me he wanted to wait before making a decision to turn his life over to Jesus. His reason? He wanted to have all his fun first! Over the years, I have wondered if he made the right decision, or if, instead, he waited too long.

It's important to remember two things about all of this. First, Paul said that *today is the day of salvation (II Corinthians 6:2).* Secondly, Jesus reminds us that no one comes to the Father except through Him (John14:6).

Hell Is Not to Be Taken Lightly

So, for the sake of each person, now in this life and in terms of eternity, I want to speak clearly. I am appalled at the careless expressions attached to the word "hell." Some of these are: "Hell, no!" and "Hell, yes!" and "What the hell!" These expressions tend to diminish the indescribable, horrific reality of hell in the minds of those who desperately need to know the truth. On and on it goes, until the word "hell" all but loses its impact. But hell is hell—a real place of fire and brimstone, a place of indescribable darkness, and a place of unimaginable suffering!

BUT GOD HIMSELF has given each of us the privilege to escape. He has put in our hands the responsibility and the opportunity to choose whether we will spend eternity in such this place called hell, or in heaven with Him. And Jesus has provided that opportunity for us. He is the Way.

SATAN IS ALIVE! And it seems that many Christians do not realize this and that we are in a spiritual war. Yet, awareness of this reality is essential in understanding our present troubles. Here are three things to remember always:

1. We need to acknowledge that Satan exists.
2. We need to understand his many tactics.
3. We need to realize that hell is a real place.

What Cannot Save Us from Hell

Pride and ignorance are probably the two main things that will keep a person from accepting the Blood of Jesus as the atonement for sin. Our best efforts to fulfil the demands of a list of rules or laws cannot save us from hell. *For whoever keeps the whole law and yet stumbles at just one point is guilty of breaking all of it (James 2:10).*

Jesus also made it clear that trying to keep the law was pointless. For preaching this, He aroused serious opposition from the keepers of the law—the scribes and Pharisees. But the truth is that only Jesus and His Blood shed at Calvary are adequate to provide for our salvation. The law cannot save. So, Jesus drew a line in the sand, so to speak, and even now, He stands by that line.

In His day, the religious leaders led God's people away from Truth. One of the main ways that they did so was by interpreting the Scriptures to suit their personal desires and ideas. In our day, some leaders still have a tendency to do this. That will never do!

Years ago, a young woman told me that I needed the Holy Spirit's fullness, but she claimed that she already had all that she needed. She was right in the sense that I was hungry for more of the Word, but her attitude reminded me of Paul's description of his fellow Jews.

> *For not knowing about God's righteousness [which is based on faith] and seeking to establish their own [righteousness based on works], they did not submit to God's righteousness. 4For Christ is the end of the law [it leads to Him and its purpose is fulfilled in Him], for [granting] righteousness to everyone who believes [in Him as Savior] (Romans 10:3-4, Amplified).*

The purpose and demands of the law to make us righteous *(i.e.,* right with God) were fulfilled, entirely and completely, by Jesus. The Bible teaches that righteousness is by faith in His finished work. Unfortunately, people are often misled from the pulpits about this and are told that they must attain righteous standing with God by their works—works such as water baptism and anything else that they suppose will assure them of salvation. It is sad that so many people are taught that they cannot enter heaven unless they fulfil prescribed religious traditions and religious rules.

The reality is that religion will actually send people to hell. In fact, Satan himself is religious. But true Christianity is not a religion. Real Christianity is a fellowship—a relationship with Our Lord.

Those who are religious, but who are outside of Christ, will know the gloomy pits of darkness described by John.

> 13*Then the sixth angel sounded: And I heard a voice from*
> *the four horns of the golden altar which is before God,*
> 14*saying to the sixth angel who had the trumpet, "Release*
> *the four angels who are bound at the great river*
> *Euphrates."* 15*So the four angels, who had been prepared*
> *for the hour and day and month and year, were released*
> *to kill a third of mankind. Wicked angels were thrown into hell, in gloomy pits of darkness and held until the day of Judgement of the wicked (Revelation 9:13-15).*

Abraham's Experience of Darkness

Abraham experienced *a great darkness* while God was making a covenant with him. This may have been a taste of the suffering his descendants would experience as slaves in Egypt, for the darkness came at the time God informed him of this future event. This darkness also brings to mind the darkness that fell on the land when Jesus was crucified.

> 9*So He said to him, Bring Me a three-year-old heifer, a three-year-old female goat, a three-year-old ram, a turtledove, and*

a young pigeon. [10]Then he brought all these to Him and cut them in two, down the middle, and placed each piece opposite the other; but he did not cut the birds in two. [11]And when the vultures came down on the carcasses, Abram drove them away (Genesis 15:9-11).

In this Old Testament passage, the heifer is a type representing the Lord Jesus. It has been pointed out that each of the animals in this passage was tame, as opposed to wild. They were servants, meeting human need. Each one foreshadowed a distinct aspect of Christ's perfection and work. Each of these animals died, of necessity, because without the shedding of blood, there is no remission of sin. (To study this in detail, see my book, *In the Beginning*).

[12]Now when the sun was going down, a deep sleep fell upon Abram; and behold, horror and great darkness fell upon him. [13]Then He said to Abram: "Know certainly that your descendants will be strangers in a land that is not theirs, and will serve them, and they will afflict them four hundred years. [14]And also the nation whom they serve I will judge; afterward they shall come out with great possessions (Genesis 15:12-14).

Darkness in the Creation Story

Light and darkness are important in the Creation narrative.

[1]In the beginning God [Elohim] created [by forming from nothing] the heavens and the earth. [2]The earth was formless and void or a waste and emptiness, and darkness was upon the face of the deep [primeval ocean that covered the unformed earth]. The Spirit of God was moving (hovering,

brooding) over the face of the waters. [3]And God said, "Let there be light"; and there was light (Genesis 3:1-3, AMP).

There are three important things I want to emphasize in this passage.

1. In the beginning, there was only darkness, emptiness, and nothingness.
2. From this nothingness, God began to create.
3. God spoke and light was created out of the darkness.

Darkness at Calvary

At Calvary, the question of sin and the claims of holiness and righteousness were forever settled. On Calvary's Cross, God's great love for us was revealed for all to see. There His judgment on sin was finalized through the death of Jesus Christ, so that, now He offers forgiveness to those who come to Him. In that forgiveness, He remembers our sins no more. The Blood has washed them away as if they had never happened. This glorious work was accomplished for us through Jesus' death on the Cross, His Resurrection, and His Ascension.

At one point in this process that provides for our salvation, darkness fell upon the earth, and that point was during the hours Jesus hung on the Cross.

[44]Now it was the sixth hour, and there was darkness over all the earth until the ninth hour. [45]Then the sun was darkened, and the veil of the temple was torn in two. [46]And when Jesus had cried out with a loud voice, He said, "Father, into Your hands I commit My spirit." Having said this, He breathed His last. [47]So when the centurion saw

what had happened, he glorified God, saying, "Certainly this was a righteous Man!" And the whole crowd who came together to that sight, seeing what had been done, beat their breasts and returned; but all His acquaintances, and the women who followed Him from Galilee, stood at a distance, watching these things (Luke 23:44-49).

In Scripture, the third hour is 9 A.M.; the sixth hour, 12 NOON; and the ninth hour, 3 P.M. From noon until 3 P.M., then, Jesus hung on the Cross in total darkness. Matthew's Gospel reports that, following this at Jesus' Resurrection, some of the Old Testament saints came out of their graves as a walking testimony of His Resurrection.

51Then, behold, the veil of the temple was torn in two from top to bottom; and the earth quaked, and the rocks were
split, 52and the graves were opened; and many bodies of
the saints who had fallen asleep were raised; 53and coming
out of the graves after His resurrection, they went into the holy city and appeared to many (Matthew 27:51-53).

"Hello, I Am Uncle Jimmy!"

My Mother had one older sister and one brother. I knew Aunt Winnie, but I had never met Uncle Jimmy. I knew he had left home to join the circus and was somewhat of a rambler. But one day he knocked on my door and introduced himself.

Uncle Jimmy stayed with me for several weeks, and during that time, I was praying for him to accept the Lord. One Sunday, I took him to church. During the altar call, I saw him grab the back of the pew in front of us and shake uncontrollably. At the time, I was much younger and did not realize that the shaking was caused by his resistance to the manifest presence of the Holy Spirit. Eventually, he managed to settle down, but the memory of that still burns in my heart today. As young and inexperienced as I was, I recognized the Lord's Voice. I knew I should not give up!

About that time, a pastor friend moved west from Irving, Texas, to the City of Eastland. That happened to be where Uncle Jimmy was living and working as an electrician. So, I called my friend, told him the story, and asked if he would reach out to him. He did, and he hired him to do some work in the church. But one day, when repair work required that Uncle Jimmy climb into the attic, he fell through the ceiling and hit the floor of the sanctuary. The pastor found him, and then and there, led him to the Lord. Uncle Jimmy joined the church and soon married a Christian lady.

I am sharing this testimony to show how tightly the lost will hold onto the benches, rather than turning loose and letting the Lord change their direction and destiny. Of course, giving up on Uncle Jimmy never occurred to me!

Our Lord would have *whosoever will* to be saved. That is why He shed His Precious Blood, and then said, "IT IS FINISHED." When the curtain ripped in the Temple from top to bottom at His death (Matthew 27:51), the *whosoever will* were liberated.

"Go, or I Will Not Send You Again!"

Several times throughout the years, the Lord has told me to do something, but I did not understand why until I had obeyed Him.

I recall, for example, how the Lord spoke firmly to me one morning as I was preparing for the day. I had been praying for a couple who had separated, and I kept telling the Lord who to send to help them. I heard the Lord say, "You go!" I said, "Oh no, Lord! Send Betty!" Then I heard these words: "Go, or I will not send you again!"

That was many years ago, and those words are still etched on my heart. I did go, and the Lord dealt with the problem they were having. They stayed together.

Chapter 6

Who Goes to Hell?

> "If there is no hell,
> let's tear down all the churches,
> and build a monument to the atheists."
>
> Billy Sunday (1862-1935)
> Celebrated American Evangelist

As we Christians study what the Bible says about hell, we become more and more aware that there is a literal, burning hell, and that it is full of unrepentant souls who chose a life of folly during their short stay here on earth.

Many times, through my years of teaching, I have told classes that Christianity is not a religion, but instead, that Christians are a people redeemed by the Blood of Jesus. We must put our faith in the saving, delivering power of the Blood of Jesus. Apart from it, we are lost, for the Word tells us *all have sinned and fallen short of the glory of God (Romans 3:23).*

The Consequences of a Terrible Deception

So, it is not the religious who go to heaven. It is followers of the Lord Jesus who spend eternity with God. With this in mind, I want to share an example of a tragic story that happened among sincere people in a cult called Christian Science. This is of special interest to me because I once asked the Lord what I should say if someone asked me if they should continue with their medicine after asking prayer for healing. The Holy Spirit said to me, "My daughter, you are not Christian Science." So, I had to understand what He meant.

The founder of Christian Science was Mary Baker Eddy (1821-1910), a false teacher. She founded the First Church of Christ Scientist and established Reading Rooms that eventually spread throughout the land.

Although she seemed to have started out with an orthodox view of God, Christ, and the Bible, she soon veered sharply away from *the faith (Jude 1:3).* Her church denies the deity of Jesus Christ and salvation through His Shed Blood. In her search for health and healing, she pursued spiritism and reportedly participated in séances.

The New Testament writers warn us to hold fast to what they call *the faith.* This refers to the basic, fundamental, and necessary doctrines of Biblical, Christian faith. Peter describes what happens to those who reject *the faith* (II Peter 2:12-13), and some do just that as they pursue their own desires.

> [7]*But the heavens and the earth which are now preserved by the same word, are reserved for fire until the day of judgment and perdition of ungodly men (2 Peter 3:7).*

Besides Christian Science, many modern cults have rejected *the faith,* replacing truth with their own pet doctrines. Here is a partial list of such doctrines that deviate from *the faith,* especially those espoused by Christian Science.

1. God is an impersonal life principle and force.
2. God is all, and all is God.

3. Matter is an illusion.
4. Jesus is not the Christ.
5. Jesus only displayed the Christ-like idea.
6. Christ means perfection and is not a person.
7. Jesus was not God, and He never became man in the flesh. He did not and could not suffer for sins.
8. Humanity is already saved.
9. Sickness is not real.
10. Jesus did not die on the Cross.

Members of the Christian Science cult rely reject modern medicine and medical doctors, relying instead on *Christian Science practitioners* instead of on medical doctors. One story of the consequences of this appeared in a 1994 edition of *Redbook Magazine*. In this article, a woman tells of having to choose between Christian Science and a physician in her efforts to save her daughter's life.

The woman stated that she had been taught that prayer, as taught by Mary Baker Eddy, could heal a person of anything and everything. But she kept seeing children in her church die because of the absence of proper medical treatment. "Finally," she said, "I could stay silent no longer." She went on to say, "When anyone passed away, they were not allowed to discuss it or mourn. It is hard to determine just how many children have died who could have been treated, but vaccines were not allowed."

When her own Mother was dying, her stomach swelled, and she suffered with excruciating pain. The practitioners told her she was not sick. When she could no longer stand the pain, she secretly went to a doctor only to discover that she had cancer. He treated her, but at some point, she refused further treatment. Finally, when the sick woman's husband decided to put her in a nursing home operated by Christian Science, they refused to admit her because she had received treatment from a medical doctor within the past year.

Later, when her own daughter became sick with terrible stomach pain, she called her practitioner who said, "She is a good child of God, and so she can't be sick. Let me assure you!" She advised, "You just need to heal your thinking."

By the fourth day, the child could not be awakened. Frantic with fear, the woman again called her practitioner. Once again, she was told that there was nothing wrong with the little girl. In desperation, the Mother took her to a doctor. At this point, she reported to her practitioner, who said, "It would have been better if you had let her die." Stunned, she said, "I hung up the phone."

The child was, in fact, suffering from a ruptured appendix. While she was about to undergo surgery to save her life, two Christian Scientist women arrived at the hospital and begged the Mother to take the child home before they could operate. At this point, the woman asked herself some serious questions. Should she impose her beliefs on her child? Could this, in fact, be a form of child abuse? Satisfied with her own analysis, she approved the operation. It was a success and the little girl regained her health.

In the end, the woman was expelled from the Christian Science Church. She said that it was great to be free and to be able to use aspirins and antibiotics when needed without having to fight a sense of guilt.

So, Where Does Hell Fit into a Person's Belief System?

Even though we may not adhere to any of the erroneous beliefs of the cults, it is still important to evaluate our stance on hell. Do we believe in a real hell? If we do not believe in a burning hell, we likely do not believe in the necessity of the Cleansing Blood of the Lamb.

We must face the fact that each of us has an eternal destiny, and where we spend eternity is our choice alone. Will we choose heaven or hell?

Near where I live in Irving, Texas, there is a Jehovah's Witness Hall (Watchtower). Often, when I pass by, I see those little children playing in the front yard before they go into the services with their parents. My heart breaks for them and for others, like them, who must follow their parents in cults.

Cults cannot meet the deep, spiritual needs of people because they are missing the Only True Source of personal redemption and reconciliation: The Lord Jesus Christ and the Blood He shed for all.

Cults peddle lies and mislead the unsuspecting and the uninformed. They deny the Trinity and the deity of Jesus Christ. They misuse God's Word and pervert the truth, and in so doing, they mislead naïve men and women.

But ignorance is no excuse! We have a personal obligation to inform ourselves, to live informed lives.

I have thought about the children and young people who were mesmerized by celebrities, such as Michael Jackson and Prince. Christian parents who paid for their children to get into their concerts may have had no idea that both men were Jehovah's Witnesses. Or perhaps they just didn't care! Some would argue that Jackson had no religion, but his family raised him and his siblings as Jehovah's Witnesses. It behooves us all to be informed.

What about Death?

> [5]*For the living know that they will die; But the dead know nothing, And they have no more reward, for the memory of them is forgotten. (Ecclesiastes 9:5)*

When do we become aware that this life on earth is not forever and that we will die one day? No one has to tell us. We just know it. But I have heard people say they will learn all they need to know after they die. No! Death is final and the decision to spend forever in heaven or hell is made on this side of the grave. It is true that the body is dead and in the grave, but our spirit never dies and will live eternally in one place or the other.

> [18]*For Sheol cannot praise or thank You, Death cannot praise You and rejoice in You; Those who go down to the pit cannot hope for Your faithfulness (Isaiah 38.18, Amplified).*

THE QUESTION IS "WHO GOES TO HELL?"
The Answer:
Those who do not come to Jesus for Salvation.

The Hebrew and Greek words for "salvation" include the ideas of deliverance, safety, preservation, soundness and healing. Dr. C. I. Scofield (1843 – 1921), best known for *The*

Scofield Bible (1909), wrote, "Salvation is the great inclusive word of the gospel, gathering into itself all the redemptive acts and processes, and justification, redemption, grace, propitiation, imputation, forgiveness, sanctification, and glorification."

No one can come to the Father except through His Son, Jesus Christ. The Holy Spirit draws, convicts, and leads us to the moment when we accept the Blood of Our Lord to cleanse us from all our iniquities and to make us new creatures in Him. Our body is then the Temple of the Holy Spirit and the Holy Spirit communicates with us through our born-again spirit. This truth is made clear in the following Scriptures.

> [23]*For I am hard-pressed between the two, having a desire to depart and be with Christ, which is far better.*
> [24]*Nevertheless to remain in the flesh is more needful for you (Philippians 1:23-24).*

> [4]*Rather let it be the hidden person of the heart, with the incorruptible beauty of a gentle and quiet spirit, which is very precious in the sight of God (1 Peter:3:4).*

> [14]*I will praise You, for I am fearfully and wonderfully made; Marvelous are Your works, And that my soul*
> *knows very well.* [15]*My frame was not hidden from You,*
> *when I was made in secret, and skillfully wrought in the*
> *lowest parts of the earth.* [16]*Your eyes saw my substance,*
> *being yet unformed, and in Your book they all were written, the days fashioned for me, when as yet there were none of them (Psalm 139:14-16).*

> *[6]For you were bought at a price; therefore glorify God in your body and in your spirit, which are God's (I Corinthians 6:20).*

Hell Is Not a Symbol

The adjective "eternal" that is used to describe the *eternal* bliss of those who are with their Father in heaven is the same adjective "eternal" that is used to describe the *eternal* state of unbelievers in hell. Both are eternal.

If we truly believe in the inerrancy of the Bible, we must embrace the reality of hell, even as Jesus Himself taught it. The late Gordon Lindsey (1906-1973) wrote that the subject of hell is a difficult subject with which to deal. I agree. And the pros and cons of doing so are ever before us. But how can we be silent about something that is so important that Jesus Himself spoke about it?

Furthermore, it is a wrong to lead people to believe that, if they choose to reject Jesus and His Shed Blood during their lifetime, that they will have a chance to accept Him once they have passed from this life. There is no Scriptural basis for the idea that we are given a second chance.

Another heresy about hell—one that is taught by some leaders who pastor large congregations—is that the Blood of Christ is not enough to provide for our salvation. They claim that Jesus had to die spiritually in hell. There is no Scriptural evidence to substantiate this teaching. It is a figment of their overactive imaginations! And because it is untrue, it can lead people straight to the gates of hell.

The facts are these. Hell is real. Hell is not a mere symbol. Hell is not a metaphor being used to explain something we do not understand by the use of something with which we are familiar. The reality is that Jesus paid the ultimate price to keep us out of the fiery pit called *hell.*

The Heart of God

> [2]*The Lord does not delay [as though He were unable to act] and is not slow about His promise, as some count slowness, but is [extraordinarily] patient toward you, not wishing for any to perish but for all to come to repentance (2 Peter 3:9, Amplified).*

Someone asked, "Why take the time to put it all together? Hell is hell!" Scriptures answer the question regarding why anyone would bother to write a book explaining the state of the lost after death. But the question really deserves no response because the Holy Spirit did not commission the inquirer to write about hell, nor did He lead that person to question why someone else should do so.

In such a situation, if one soul is led to Jesus as a result of the Biblical knowledge presented, then it will have been worth the hours invested in researching and writing. Hell is real! People must be made aware of that fact.

When a person dies, the body is placed in a grave, but the spirit and soul of that person go immediately to either heaven or hell. The spirit and soul are eternal. A spirit cannot be killed. In relation to this and to other Biblical truths that are beyond our natural understanding, we must acknowledge the Holy Spirit as *The Teacher.* We need Him to help us understand The Bible (John 16:13) and the things of the Spirit. Our natural minds are limited, and to read the Word with our natural understanding can keep us from the truth and can lead to heresy.

The Parable of the Wheat and the Tares

Matthew records a story that Jesus used to teach about two groups of people: authentic believers and pretenders. The story is called *The Parable of the Wheat and the Tares (Matthew 13:24-43).* The *wheat* represents those who are true followers of Jesus, and the *tares* represent those who, for whatever reason, are not true disciples. Jesus explains that the wheat and the tares will grow alongside one another until harvest time, and that, in the same way, the real and the counterfeit will be together in this world until His Return.

> 24*Another parable He put forth to them, saying: "The kingdom of heaven is like a man who sowed good seed in his field;* 25*but while men slept, his enemy came and sowed tares among the wheat and went his way.* 26*But when the grain had sprouted and produced a crop, then the tares also appeared.* 27*So the servants of the owner came and said to him, 'Sir, did you not sow good seed in your field? How then does it have tares?'* 28*He said to them, 'An enemy has done this.' The servants said to him, 'Do you want us then to go and gather them up?'* 29*But he said, 'No, lest while you gather up the tares you also uproot the wheat with them.* 30*Let both grow together until the harvest, and at the time of harvest I will say to the reapers, 'First gather together the tares and bind them in bundles to burn them, but gather the wheat into my barn'" (Matthew 13:24-30).*

Matthew tells what Jesus said when His Disciples approached Him in private, asking Him to explain the parable.

> 37"*He who sows the good seed is the Son of Man.* 38*The*
> *field is the world, the good seeds are the sons of the*
> *kingdom, but the tares are the sons of the wicked one.*
> 39*The enemy who sowed them is the devil, the harvest is*
> *the end of the age, and the reapers are the angels.*
> 40*Therefore as the tares are gathered and burned in the*
> *fire, so it will be at the end of this age.* 41*The Son of Man*
> *will send out His angels, and they will gather out of His*
> *kingdom all things that offend, and those who practice*
> *lawlessness,* 42*and will cast them into the furnace of fire.*
> *There will be wailing and gnashing of teeth.* 43*Then the*
> *righteous will shine forth as the sun in the kingdom of*
> *their Father. He who has ears to hear, let him hear!"*
> *(Matthew 13:36-43).*

In this parable, *the field* is not the church; it is the world. The wheat, representing those who believe in Him, He calls *children of the kingdom.* The tares, those representing those who do not believe in Him, He calls *children of the wicked one.*

This parable is about the Kingdom of Heaven. In the story, the landowner specifically tells his servants not to pull up the weeds growing in the field, but instead, to let them continue to live and grow until the end of the age. The enemy who sowed the bad seed is Satan, whose efforts are designed to destroy Christ's work through false believers and false teachers who lead many away from Truth.

Jesus' parable is certainly confirmed in our day. Although many leaders are faithful shepherds and many believers are authentic disciples of the Lord, there are those among us who are neither. From time to time, the exposure of the latest scandals by televangelists and other church leaders reveals the existence of tares whose actions bring reproach to the name of Christ. Jesus explains that the angels will separate them from the wheat at harvest time and that they will be thrown into the fires of hell. That, I contend, goes a long way in answering the question as to who will be in hell.

Matthew 28:16-20 makes our assignment clear. Our job is to go into the world to proclaim and teach *The Good News* that Jesus saves. Earlier in this chapter, we shared a list of those who would not go to heaven, but who will, instead spend eternity in hell. I want to elaborate on that.

Homosexuality Is Condemned in Scripture

In 2015, the United States Supreme Court legalized same-sex marriage. It is important to remember that legalization of this or anything else by a human court does not overrule the law of God. God calls homosexuality an abomination. It is a lifestyle that is contrary both to how He created human beings and to the Creation model of marriage and sexuality. God's will about this is clearly spelled out in Leviticus 18:22; 20:13 and Romans 1:26-27.

Leviticus 18:22-24 provides a list of abominations together with explicit commands against such acts. These include the following:

1. Do not lie with man as with a woman (vs. 22).
2. Do not lie with a beast (vs. 23).
3. Neither shall a woman lie with a beast (vs. 23).

4. *'Do not defile yourselves with any of these things; for by all these the nations are defiled, which I am casting out before you (vs. 24).*

God warned that disobedience would bring destruction to the land. He said, *I will visit the punishment of iniquity upon it, and the land vomits out its inhabitants (Leviticus 18:25).*

The sinful acts listed in this passage are characteristic of pagan worship. The punishment allotted is mentioned in verse 29: *For whoever commits any of these abominations, the persons who commit them shall be cut off from among their people.* That should be clearly understood to mean that hell is waiting for those who disobey in this manner.

This issue is also addressed in the New Testament. Paul says that *God gave them up (Romans 1:24).* He reiterates this in verses 26 and 28, where he writes, *God gave them over.* In this statement, Paul is referring to the homosexual act, and he seems to see it as the epitome of sexual sin.

The expression "sin of sodomy" is derived from what was happening in the City of Sodom (Genesis 19). Because of the pervasive practice of homosexuality in that city, God announces that He will destroy Sodom. Abraham was especially concerned because his nephew Lot lived in there.

> [1]*Now the two angels came to Sodom in the evening, and Lot was sitting in the gate of Sodom. When Lot saw them, he rose to meet them, and he bowed himself with his face toward the ground.*
> [2]*And he said, "Here now, my lords, please turn in to your servant's house and spend the night, and wash your feet; then you may rise early and go on your way . . . Now before they lay down, the men of*

the city, the men of Sodom, both old and young, all the people from every quarter, surrounded the house. [5]And they called to Lot and said to him, "Where are the men who came to you tonight? Bring them out to us that we may know them carnally" (Genesis 19:1-4).

Several years ago, I heard a preacher teaching about the so-called "'Gay Movement' coming out of the closet," and he mentioned something that I sensed was straight from the Lord. He said that in the early 1970s, the Gay Movement was just beginning to gain popularity, noting that this surge paralleled the deadly AIDS outbreak. But the band played on! With many still dying from HIV, it makes me wonder what it will take to wake up America!

In reading an article about binding the homosexual spirit, I noticed that the author did not distinguish between "binding" and "deliverance." Deliverance is, in fact, the only way out of the demonic lifestyle of homosexuality. It must be acknowledged that it is a sin and an abomination in the sight of God, and counselling is not the answer. Deliverance is. And today's cry of *Love the sinner but hate the sin!* is not the Word of God. Some claim that the statement originated with Gandhi. It provides no way out for the sinner who is bound in a sinful lifestyle. There is a way out of this lifestyle, and it is through the Blood of Jesus and the Word of God.

To understand this fully requires that we go back to Genesis where it all began. There we learn of this sin, but we also learn of God's Covenant with His people. He is a covenant-keeping God, and that makes all the difference. He does not break covenant just because we sin.

For those who have repented, turned from a homosexual lifestyle, and put their faith in Jesus, it is important to know that, despite being saved, the possibility of struggling with feelings and temptation may persist. That does not mean that the repentant person is not saved. In the story of *The Prodigal Son (Luke 15:1-7),* when the man left the pigpen and headed for his Father's house, he probably had manure on his shoes, straw in his hair, and the smell of the pigpen on him. What made the difference was that he had left the pigpen and was on his way home.

Be sure that you have left the pigpens of sin.

If you are one of those who lives in condemnation after you have received Jesus, know that it not God who is testing or tempting you. It is the devil trying to destroy you. The mind is his playground. When you choose to put your faith in Jesus, the devil knows he has lost your spirit to the Creator of the Universe! But he will never stop trying to intimidate you as long as you allow it.

> If we live as if this life is to go on forever, we are living in delusion, and the devil is preparing a special place for those who live with the motto: *Eat, Drink, and Be Merry.*

Chapter 7

Witchcraft

> *So Samuel said: "Has the* LORD *as great delight in burnt offerings and sacrifices, as in obeying the voice of the* LORD*? Behold, to obey is better than sacrifice, And to heed than the fat of rams.* [23]*For rebellion is as the sin of witchcraft, and stubbornness is as iniquity and idolatry."*
>
> 1 Samuel 15:22-23

It would be better to sit eternally in a lighted corner of heaven, experiencing the peace and joy of the Presence of God, than to spend one hour in the darkness of hell, listening to cries of torment and gnashing of teeth. One writer stated that Jude's message about the inhabitants of Sodom and Gomorrah *suffering the vengeance of eternal fire (Jude 7)* is clear and "rings like [the wake-up alarm] of a three-fold trumpet blast!"

Some people who do not believe in hell base their position on the idea that the body could not burn eternally. At some point, they maintain, it would have to be consumed. But that is the point at which those who hold this position are thinking in terms of the natural realm. But God supersedes the natural. He created the Universe. He is so far beyond us! So, He knows how it is that a human body can burn in hell forever. It is a small thing for Him!

In dealing with issues like this—thinking about things that are beyond our natural comprehension—it is important not to speculate where the Scriptures are silent. The thing to know is that those who are saved will receive a glorified body. Likewise, at some point, the unsaved will receive a body that never dies, and it will burn in hell eternally.

Spiritual Warfare

It is quite amazing how often we Christians so often fail to praise our way out of a pit or trap that Satan has skillfully set for us. Even though libraries are full of books on our authority over the devil and his cohorts, many Christians seem to know little about how to walk victoriously in the midst of these attacks. The story of Saul's disobedience can be very enlightening in this regard.

The problem had arisen when Samuel the Prophet was old, and his two sons were not walking in the ways of the Lord. As a result, the people became restless and demanded a king. God warned them about the consequences of this, but they insisted, and so, He gave them what they wanted. He chose a tall, handsome man named Saul from the tribe of Benjamin to be their king. He then providentially arranged for Samuel to anoint him as king. It happened this way.

One day, Saul's father sent him to find his lost donkeys. The search led Saul to the land of Zuph where he sought advice from Samuel, the man of God (I Samuel 9:5). God had alerted Samuel in advance.

> [15]*Now the Lord had told Samuel in his ear a day before Saul came, saying,* [16]*To morrow about this time I will send thee a man out of the land of Benjamin, and thou*

> *shalt anoint him to be captain over my people Israel, that he may save my people out of the hand of the Philistines: for I have looked upon my people, because their cry is come unto me.* [17]*And when Samuel saw Saul, the Lord said unto him, Behold the man whom I spake to thee of! (I Samuel 9:15-17).*

Samuel invited Saul to eat with him and to stay overnight. The next morning, before sending him on his way, Samuel told Saul to send his companions on ahead, leaving the two alone so that Samuel could tell Saul God's plans for him. Samuel then anointed him King of Israel.

As King Saul's life unfolds, it reveals one of the most vivid stories of total disobedience reported in the Word of God. He fell so far that, in the latter part of his life, he could no longer hear the Voice of God, and in desperation, he turned to a witch for direction.

The Impact of King Saul's Disobedience

Later through Samuel, God commanded Saul to destroy the Amalekites completely and to kill their sheep and cattle (I Samuel 15). Nothing was to be left of the Amalekites. This may seem harsh, but the Amalekites had attacked and oppressed God's people from the time He had delivered them out of Egypt. Also, it is helpful to remember that the Amalekites are an Old Testament picture of Satan and his demons and their attacks on God's New Covenant people.

Many years prior to this, God had spoken to Moses about the Amalekites and their total annihilation.

[17]Remember what the Amalekites did to you along the way when you came out of Egypt. [18]When you were weary and worn out, they met you on your journey and attacked all who were lagging behind; they had no fear of God. [19]When the LORD your God gives you rest from all the enemies around you in the land he is giving you to possess as an inheritance, you shall blot out the name of Amalek from under heaven. Do not forget! (Deuteronomy 25:17-19, NIV).

So, this command through Samuel to Saul was to be the fulfillment of the command that God had given Moses. But Saul disobeyed. When he saw the sheep and cattle, he decided to keep the best of them. He also spared Agag, the King of the Amalekites.

When Samuel confronted Saul about his disobedience, Saul immediately sought to justify himself, saying to Samuel, *Blessed are you of the Lord! I have performed the commandment of the Lord (I Samuel 15:13).* Samuel replied, *What then is this bleating of the sheep in my ears and the lowing of the oxen which I hear? (I Samuel 15:14).*

Still seeking to justify himself, Saul replied,

[15]They have brought them from the Amalekites: for the people spared the best of the sheep and of the oxen, to sacrifice unto the Lord thy God; and the rest we have utterly destroyed (I Samuel 15:15).

But this was just an excuse and not the real reason that Saul had spared the best of the sheep and cattle. At this point, Samuel responded with the words that are the theme of this chapter. He said to Saul,

[22]Has the LORD as great delight in burnt offerings and sacrifices, as in obeying the voice of the LORD? Behold to obey is better than sacrifice, and to heed than the fat of rams. [23]For rebellion is as the sin of witchcraft, and stubbornness is as iniquity and idolatry. Because you have rejected the word of the LORD, He has also rejected you from being king (I Samuel 15:22-23).

This story is a prime example of what happens when a person disobeys the Lord's commands. Along with the disobedience, comes lying to cover up the sin. Sin follows the unrepentant sinner, as this story shows.

When King Saul begged for forgiveness, Samuel told him that God would depart from him, for he had rejected the Word of the Lord. He also told Saul that the Lord had rejected him as King. At this point, Samuel turned to go, and as he did, Saul seized the edge of Samuel's robe, and it tore. That ripping was symbolic confirmation that He had rejected Saul as King, for it was a signal that the kingdom had been torn from him.

From that point on, Saul could no longer hear the Voice of the Lord.

Sometime later, when a massive Philistine army gathered to destroy Israel, in an attempt to get direction, Saul sought the advice of the Witch of Endor, a woman with a familiar spirit (I Samuel 28:7-25). The woman conjured up a figure, supposedly from the dead, who claimed to be Samuel and who confirmed what Samuel had told him; that is, that God had departed from him and the kingdom had been given to David. He also told Saul that he and his sons would die the next day in battle. It happened exactly as was foretold.

Our purpose is not to discuss whether or not the figure conjured up by the witch was actually Samuel or a demonic manifestation. Instead, our purpose is to show how Saul's stubborn disobedience led to his losing the blessing and the ability to commune with God. His disobedience also shows the connection between rebellion and witchcraft. It points to the fact that our obedience to the Lord is important, and that it brings with it God's peace.

This Is Not a Game

The late Lester Sumrall (1913-1996) made the following statement in reference to his book on demons entitled *Alien Entities*: "I don't normally make this confession, but I have suffered more as a result of teaching what you are reading right now than for anything in my entire life."

Like many Christians of his day, Dr. Sumrall grew up in a fundamentalist, evangelical church that did not inform its people about the devil or witchcraft. So, when he began teaching these things, they made fun of him and often referred to Satan as *Old Slew Foot.* In fact, this name is a reference to the devil commonly used in Colonial America (1607-1776). In what the people thought was an effort not to draw the devil's attention, they referred to him by various names. This particular name—*Old Slew Foot*—refers to the notion that his feet had no toes and resembled hooves.

Dr. Sumrall cautioned his fellow evangelicals to be wise regarding the devil and his tactics. He also warned them to be careful in their choice of words and references because his schemes to destroy people are not a joke!

If, in ignorance, we take the devil lightly, he will not heed our commands to stop his attacks. He does not respect our jokes and ridicule.

Recently, I heard someone use the expression "holy hell." I thought about it for a moment and wondered what could possibly be holy about hell.

And as a young person, I remember hearing people mock Full Gospel people because they talked about the devil. That's unfortunate because the devil is a powerful enemy who does not want to be exposed. One avenue that he uses is witchcraft, and it is on the rise in this country and around the world.

What is Witchcraft?

There are only two sources of supernatural power on earth: the power of God and the evil power of Satan. Any power beyond the natural comes from either God or the devil. But it is important to remember that God's power far surpasses any that the devil might have. God is supreme.

What is witchcraft and where does it derive its power? It has been defined as "knowledge beyond our human understanding," but that is not a true and adequate definition. Basically, witchcraft employs various means and methods in an effort to control people and circumstances. According to the *Collins English Dictionary,* witchcraft is: 1) the art or power of bringing magical . . . power to bear or the act or practice of attempting to do so; 2) the influence of magic or sorcery. And according to Galatians 5:20, witchcraft is a *work of the flesh,* as opposed to a spiritual empowerment with its source in God (Galatians 5:22-23).

Witchcraft is often practiced by using such items as crystal balls, Ouija boards, the Enneagram, and by engaging in rituals such as séances and spellcasting. It also involves fortune telling, divining the future, and necromancy. Scripture clearly forbids these pagan practices.

> [9]*When thou art come into the land which the Lord thy God giveth thee, thou shalt not learn to do after the abominations of those nations.*
>
> [10]*There shall not be found among you anyone that maketh his son or his daughter to pass through the fire, or that useth divination, or an observer of times, or an enchanter, or a witch.*
>
> [11]*Or a charmer, or a consulter with familiar spirits, or a wizard, or a necromancer.*
>
> [12]*For all that do these things are an abomination unto the Lord: and because of these abominations the Lord thy God doth drive them out from before thee (Deuteronomy 18:9-12, KJV).*

The Merriam-Webster Dictionary defines *necromancy* as "the conjuration of the spirits of the dead for purposes of magically revealing the future or influencing the course of events." People grieving over a departed loved one might be vulnerable to this practice, but it can put a person in the clutches of the devil.

Isaiah warns against seeking knowledge from witches.

> *And when they say to you, "Seek those who are mediums*

> *and wizards, who whisper and mutter," should not a people seek their God? Should they seek the dead on behalf of the living? To the law and the testimony! If they do not speak according to this word, it is because there is no light in them (Isaiah 8:19-20).*

Paul warns against what he calls *fellowship with devils.*

> [20]*But I say that the things which the Gentiles sacrifice, they sacrifice to devils, and not to God: and I would not that ye should have fellowship with devils. (I Corinthians 10:20)*

Dabbling in the occult by any of its various means and methods is dangerous. It involves calling forth another power to control our lives and the lives of others.

Something to remember, too, is that when members of a household do not understand the wiles of the devil, it seems that even one person in that household can open the door of destruction to others in the household. So, every generation must be alerted to this danger and must be taught the Truth.

Idolatry Forbidden

Paul notes that witchcraft is a work of the flesh, along with *adultery, fornication, uncleanness, lewdness (Galatians 5:19-20).* Involvement begins with a natural, human desire for power and control, and it is willing to tap into evil forces to obtain that power and control.

Satan wants to gain control, and the process is clear. It is three-fold. He first intimidates, and then he manipulates.

Once he is successful in these two tactics, he proceeds to dominate. This process is certainly obvious in witchcraft.

1. Intimidation
2. Manipulation
3. Domination

When people even so much as dabble in witchcraft, they are setting themselves up for loss and death. Jesus words ring true:

> *The thief does not come except to steal, and to kill, and to destroy. I have* come *that they may have life, and that they may have it more abundantly (John 10:10).*

Acts of witchcraft open the door in a person's life to the supernatural control and destructive power of Satan. But God has given us His Word, His Blood, and His Name as weapons against such demonic devices. While devils are on assignment to steal, kill and destroy us, Our Lord is greater, and He has given us the tools for victory in Him.

Plead The Blood!

Shortly after I had received the infilling of the Holy Spirit, I was challenged by the devil. At the time, I knew so little about the Holy Spirit! For example, I thought that once I received my prayer language—like that of my friends and those I had heard speaking in tongues in church—I would never be sick again.

At this time, I was teaching seventh-grade English. At the same time every year, I would come down with strep throat, and only a shot of antibiotics would cure me. Knowing I would get sick, I would make out my instruction sheets for a substitute teacher. It wasn't long before I was hit with it. (At this time, I was new to the things of the Holy Spirit.)

The pain was so intense that I cried that night. I told the Lord I would take just one aspirin. By the grace of God, I finally fell asleep. The next morning, I was up with my Bible in hand, and about all I knew about healing were a couple of verses in Isaiah 53.

> [4]*Surely he hath borne our griefs, and carried our sorrows: yet we did esteem him stricken, smitten of God, and afflicted.* [5]*But he was wounded for our transgressions, he was bruised for our iniquities: the chastisement of our peace was upon him; and with his stripes we are healed (Isaiah 53:4-5).*

I opened the Bible and told the Lord, based on this passage, that He had let me down. I held up His Word and with tears in my eyes, I read that passage to Him. Suddenly, a lump came into my throat! I felt a spirit of fear! So, I said to the Lord, "Well, I smarted off to You! I guess I will see You in a minute." Just then, a miracle happened. I heard the Lord whisper to me, "Plead the Blood." I did and the knot in my throat dissolved. I had a supernatural healing!

The Spirit of Sorcery

Sorcery is so closely associated with witchcraft that the two can be said to be synonymous, for all intents and purposes. Modern practitioners claim that the difference between the two is motive. They claim that sorcery uses magical powers to cause harm, while witchcraft seeks good in its use of magic. Regardless of modern definitions, God's Word condemns both.

The word "sorcery" is a translation of the Greek word *pharmakeion,* from which we also get the English word "pharmacy." *Thayer's Greek-English Lexicon* defines the word *pharmakeion* as "the administering of drugs" and "poisoning." It also defines the word as "sorcery" and "magical arts."

This definition shows clearly that the drug culture of our day is sorcery at work trying to capture the souls of an entire generation. In this culture, psychedelic drugs are used to produce an altered state of consciousness in the belief that they can, thereby, tap into another realm or level of existence.

There Is Freedom in Jesus

It is heart-breaking to see the great need for deliverance among God's people! And surely, the desire to set men, women, and children free from the grip of Satan is from the very Heart of God.

Several years ago, I was ministering at a women's retreat and I encountered a woman who needed deliverance. This woman was a young mother of three. She was helped to the prayer line by a woman who explained that she was subject to seizures, and although she had been under the care of a therapist, she was no better.

The Holy Spirit immediately alerted me that she was under the influence of demons. I had been in the ministry long enough to know not to lay empty hands on her. I sought the Lord about what to do. He showed me that she was experiencing demonic attacks, and that she had opened herself to these through her heavy work schedule at home, added to the demands of her responsibilities in the church.

As I ministered to her, the Holy Spirit rose up in me and what I experienced felt like a great storm breaking forth. I laid my hands on her, and before I could do no more than call on the Blood of Jesus for her deliverance, she hit the floor. They carried her out and put her to bed. Before I left the next day, the group told me that that she had slept for the rest of the day and throughout the night and that she was totally delivered.

A Word of Warning about Music

I want to tell about an experience I had in delivering a teenage girl from demonic activity brought on by the music being used in the church she attended. Yes, music can open the door to demonic activity, and so I want to encourage every leader to be wise regarding music. For example, forbid music with the beat that encourages gyrations and unholy, suggestive physical movements.

The girl was about fifteen years old at the time, and the church music that had entrapped her was suggestive music that had an erotic beat. The girl's Mother led me to her bedroom, and there she was on the floor, moving in all sorts of suggestive ways. It was obvious that this was indecent and was not a response to the Spirit of God.

Confronting her daughter, the Mother said, "I told you that was not the Lord!" One command in Jesus' Name, claiming the Power of His Blood, set the girl free. She was on her feet, no longer under the control of demonic powers.

Satan's Power Operates Through Witchcraft

Several years ago, a self-professed witch in the United States Air Force asked for and was granted Halloween off as a religious holiday. Then, there is the report of another self-professing witch in El Paso, Texas, who bragged about giving up her baby at birth to a Satanic group for human sacrifice. She said, "It was an honor to sacrifice my baby to Lord Satan." Even more bizarre is the movement of those who profess to be Christian witches. Witchcraft is alive and well in the world today.

Well-known pastor John Hagee (b. 1940) noted, "God's power manifested upon the earth operates through the Holy Spirit. Satan's power manifested upon the earth operates through the spirit of witchcraft."

No one can have two masters. We either serve the Lord or we are under the control of witchcraft in some way. When the authority of God is rejected, the spirit of witchcraft is in charge.

Rebellion and witchcraft go hand-in-hand. Remember the story of King Saul and be aware that the practice of witchcraft is condemned by God. NOTHING BUT THE BLOOD OF JESUS SETS US FREE!

Chapter 8

The Devil and His Angels

> *Then He will also say to those on the left hand, "Depart from Me, you cursed, into everlasting fire prepared for the devil and his angels."*
> *Matthew 25:41*

The Greek word translated "angel" in Scripture is *angelos* and can mean "messenger." Most of the time, it refers to heavenly messengers, such as Gabriel, who carry messages from God to earthly recipients, as he did to Mary (Luke 1:26-38). But *angelos* can also refer to a human messenger. For example, John the Baptist is referred to as God's *angelos,* or *messenger* (Matthew 11:10).

With this in mind, we should look again at something Jesus said:

> *Then He will also say to those on the left hand, "Depart from Me, you cursed, into everlasting fire prepared for the devil and his angels" (Matthew 25:41).*

The possibility is that Jesus' reference to the devil and his angels could be translated *the devil and his messengers.* It also opens the possibility that the messengers may include humans who act, perhaps unwittingly, as the devil's agents, spreading his lies and falsehoods.

In understanding these things, it is important to keep in mind that Christianity is not a religion. It is a relationship. It is fellowship with God, Our Creator and with Jesus whom Matthew calls *Immanuel,* meaning *God With Us (Matthew 1:23).* Jesus shed His Precious Blood to set us free from Satan's grip, but in this relationship, the flesh fights against the spirit, and the spirit against the flesh (Galatians 5:17). Our choices determine which prevails: Will we be controlled by our flesh or will we be led by the Spirit?

The late Chuck Smith (1927-2013), founder of the Calvary Chapel Movement, had some thoughts about this. He noted that, in this battle, the mind is always in the middle. If flesh is ruling, he said that fellowship with God is broken. He goes on to explain that when God created Adam, He created spirit, soul, and body, and since God is Spirit, our connection with Him is our spirit part. *They that worship Him must worship Him in spirit and truth (John 4:24).*

While our soul and body relate and function through our five senses, our spirit is that part of us that relates to the Lord. It could be said that our body and soul give us *world-consciousness,* while our spirit gives us *God-consciousness.*

Satan wants us to operate according to our body and soul—that is, our flesh. He does not want us to operate by our spirit, taking our cues from the Holy Spirit. He knows that when we operate in the flesh, we tend to make bad decisions that bring harm to us and others.

Along these lines, I have been intrigued by the stories of two well-known people in my lifetime. One is Aristotle Onassis (1906-1975) and the other is Karla Fay Tucker (1959-1998). Both individuals captured my attention, as well as the attention of millions around the world. Their lives differed greatly from one another, and so did their final ends. One died trusting an idol; the other, trusting Jesus.

Aristotle Onassis

Aristotle Onassis was a shipping magnate who amassed the world's largest privately owned shipping fleet and who was one of the world's richest and most famous men. Among his exploits was his 1968 marriage to Jacqueline Kennedy (1929-1994), widow of American President John F. Kennedy (1917-1963).

Onassis was born in Smyrna in modern-day Turkey in 1906. In 1922, he and his family moved to Greece to escape war. In 1923, he moved to Argentina where he began to amass his huge fortune. Later, he relocated to Monaco, where he gained economic control of this gambling capital. Through the decades, he continued to expand his economic empire, so that, when he died in 1975, he had a net worth of $500 million.

His marriage to Jackie Kennedy drew world-wide attention, with the masses glued to their television sets watching the wedding ceremony. Sometime later, he made the interesting remark that she spent too much money shopping.

The story surrounding his death is one of the saddest reports that I have ever watched on television. When he was on his deathbed, his family sent a plane to Rome to retrieve an image of the Virgin Mary in the hopes that this idol would restore his health.

I stayed abreast of events during the three days that it took for the image to reach his bedside. I kept saying to myself, "Don't they know that Mary has no power to heal? It is the Blood of Jesus. Meet Him at the Cross!"

Obviously, I was not present at his death, so I cannot say exactly what happened, but I suspect that he passed into darkness, clutching a dead idol.

Karla Faye Tucker

Karla Faye Tucker was born in 1959 in Houston, Texas, where she grew up in a troubled home. By the time she was 12 years old, she was taking drugs and having sex, and when she was 14, she dropped out of school and followed her Mother into prostitution.

Then, in 1983, under the influence of drugs, she and Danny Garrett murdered Jerry Dean and Deborah Ruth Thornton with a three-foot pickaxe in Dean's Houston apartment. Five weeks after the murders, they were arrested and indicted. While in jail awaiting trial, she took a Bible from the prison ministry program and read it in her cell. She later recalled, "I didn't know what I was reading. Before I knew it, I was in the middle of my cell floor on my knees. I was just asking God to forgive me." She became a Christian in October 1983, and in 1995, she married her prison chaplain.

It was unusual for the death penalty to be sought for female murderers in Texas, but in 1984, she was sentenced to death. Between that time and 1992, her many requests for a retrial and appeals were denied. Her plea garnered widespread support, including from such sources as the United Nations Commissioner, the World Council of Churches, Pope John

Paul II, Newt Gingrich who was, at the time, the Speaker of the U.S. House of Representatives, and televangelist Pat Robertson. The warden of Texas' Huntsville Prison testified that she was a model prisoner and that, after 14 years on death row, she likely had been reformed. Despite all of this support, Texas Governor George W. Bush refused to grant her request, and on February 3, 1998, she was executed. Her last words were:

> I would like to say to all of you—the Thornton family and Jerry Dean's family—that I am so sorry. I hope God will give you peace with this. [She looked at her husband.] Baby, I love you. [She looked at Ronald Carlson.] Ron, give Peggy a hug for me. [She looked at all present weeping and smiling.] Everybody has been so good to me. I love all of you very much. I am going to be face to face with Jesus now. Warden Baggett, thank all of you so much. You have been so good to me. I love all of you very much. I will see you all when you get there. I will wait for you.
>
> As the deadly chemicals were being administered, she praised Jesus Christ, ... looked at the ceiling, and hummed. She was pronounced dead ... eight minutes after receiving the injection. She was buried at Forest Park Lawndale Cemetery in Houston.

The two stories—Aristotle Onassis' and Karla Fay's—were so different. One shows a rich man dying, while clutching a vain idol. The other shows a happy Christian at peace, dying by lethal injection.

Never exalt a sin above the Blood of the Lamb.

We Are in a Battle

Countless books have been written and thousands of sermons have been preached on the reality of the devil and his demons. In his first epistle, Peter warns us to be alert concerning his devices: *Be sober, be vigilant; because your adversary the devil walks about like a roaring lion, seeking whom he may devour (1 Peter 5:6-8).* Despite this warning, the Church seems to do little to stop his efforts to entrap people.

Has the Church gone to sleep when it comes to the demonic world? Does the Church not understand that the devil is ruthless, and that he has no capacity to love, nor to show mercy? He is an adversary—an enemy through and through! When he has a victim cornered in his ongoing efforts to steal, kill, and destroy, he dares to roar in the face of God: "We have another one!"

There is only one devil, and the Greek word for "devil" is *diablos*. In fact, he has many names, including *Devil* and *Satan*. He is *the god of this Age,* and his mission is summed up by John: *The thief does not come except to steal, and to kill, and to destroy (John 10:10).*

Jesus' mission is just the opposite: *I am come that they might have life, and that they might have it more abundantly. I am the good shepherd: the good shepherd giveth his life for the sheep (John 10:10b-11).*

Paying Attention to the Holy Spirit

A few years ago, I was on an American Airlines flight headed for Phoenix to speak in an evening service. Usually, I would leave a day early in order to rest and study, but in this case, I felt that the Lord urged me to change my flight. By the time my Dallas flight arrived at Houston's Hobby Airport, a heavy storm grounded us. We boarded, but the captain announced that we could not fly until the storm had passed.

I was seated next to a young Catholic lady who was on her way to meet her boyfriend in Phoenix, and they were to plan their wedding. I told her about my work for the Lord and we were enjoying each other's conversation when the captain announced that we were going to take off and fly above the storm.

The Lord spoke to my heart and told me to pray. As He spoke, it felt as if a storm was hitting my heart. I told my new friend not to talk to me because the Lord had told me to pray. She became quiet and remained very still. Silently I prayed. In a little bit, the captain came on again and announced: "I thought you might like to know that, after we lifted up, a heavy lightning bolt hit the very spot on the tarmac where we had been sitting."

That young lady said, for all to hear: "You better be glad we have a praying lady on this plane. God told her to pray!" I was not embarrassed. I was rejoicing in my heart that God used me to stop the destructive work the devil had planned for that flight. God turned the situation around for good.

This testimony serves to remind us that we are fighting a spiritual battle with the enemy every day, but that Jesus has already won the victory for us on Calvary with His Precious Blood.

It has been suggested that Satan exercises power from *the*

second heaven (i.e., the principalities and powers mentioned in Ephesians 3:10; 6:12), while God is in control from *the third heaven* mentioned by Paul in II Corinthians 12:2.

When Satan gives his orders, God overrules them. Satan and God are not equal in any respect, including in spiritual warfare. But our decisions also enter the picture. God wants us, His church, to exercise the authority He has delegated to us to destroy the works of the devil and his cohorts. There are times when the Lord wants to alert us to danger, and we must be attentive always to respond to His nudging. To do this, we must know Him.

Scripture tells us that God wants us to know Him and His ways. Luke writes: *Known to God from eternity are all His ways (Acts 15:18).* The Psalmist writes: *He made known His ways to Moses, His acts to the children of Israel (Psalm 103:7).* God said of Abraham: *For I have known him, in order that he may command his children and his household after him, that they keep the way of the LORD (Genesis 18:19).*

We can have a real relationship with the Lord. In that relationship, we can get to know Him and to understand His ways. And although countless stories attest to this, Scriptures warns us that we, like Jesus, will be tempted to leave God's ways.

Avenues of Temptation

In his first epistle, John points out the three avenues the devil uses to tempt the children of God: the lust of the flesh, the lust of the eyes, and the pride of life.

> *For all that is in the world—the lust of the flesh, the lust*

of the eyes, and the pride of life—is not of the Father but is of the world (I John 2:16).

The late John Osteen (1921-1999) was a great communicator, and he made an interesting observation that gives us a helpful picture of the attacks of Satan. He said, "From our birth, the devil starts a file on us, and he endeavors to build it, so it is no surprise that he knows our weaknesses."

Our enemy, Satan, is a very real spirit person and not just a myth or figment of human imagination. His kingdom is one of darkness and lies. He will never tell us the truth. It is also true that he does not have access to our born-again spirit. But he does work through the soul realm: the mind, the will, and the emotions.

Our sure defense arises from our diligent study of God's Word, making us wise and helping us distinguish between what is of God and what is the devil's doing. When the devil and his demons put a thought into our minds, the outcome depends on what we do with it. We can learn about this from Jesus' example in Matthew 4:1-11.

This passage explains that the devil tempted Jesus in three different areas, and Jesus' responses show us how we are to respond when the devil attempts to dominate us.

It is the devil—not God—who tempted Jesus. It is true that Jesus was led into the wilderness by the Holy Spirit, but it was the devil who did the tempting. The Lord does not tempt His children. *When tempted, no one should say, "God is tempting me." For God cannot be tempted by evil, nor does he tempt anyone (James 1:13, NIV).*

How Jesus Overcame the Devil's Devices

Jesus' approach to overcoming the devil's tactics is the same way that we are to overcome. Regardless of the specific nature of the temptation, it will fall into one of three categories.

The first avenue of temptation against Jesus involved *the lust of the flesh.* So, Satan made his first attack on what he considered the Lord's weakest point to be after a long fast.

> [1]*Then Jesus was led up by the Spirit into the wilderness*
> *to be tempted by the devil.* [2]*And when He had fasted forty*
> *days and forty nights, afterward He was hungry.* [3]*Now*
> *when the tempter came to Him, he said, "If You are the Son of God, command that these stones become bread" (Matthew 4:1-3).*

Some translators contend that the word "if" in verse 3 should be rendered "since," but the evidence points to "if" as being the better choice.

Verse 3 also shows the devil's efforts to cast doubt on Jesus' identity as God's Son. In the same way, when we are born again, the devil tries to get us to doubt our new identity as children of God.

Jesus overcame the devil by countering with the Written Word of God. For Jesus, this was the highest authority. It is also the highest authority for us.

> *But He answered and said, "It is written, 'Man shall not live by bread alone, but by every word that proceeds from the mouth of God'" (Matthew 4:4).*

The second temptation involved *the pride of life.*

> [5]*Then the devil took Him up into the holy city, set Him*

on the pinnacle of the temple, [6]and said to Him, "If You are the Son of God, throw Yourself down. For it is written: "He shall give His angels charge over you, and in their hands they shall bear you up, lest you dash your foot against a stone" (Matthew 4:5-6).

The devil tempted Jesus to do something sensational and dramatic—to put on a show and to draw attention to Himself. "Climb to the top of the temple! Leap off! Claim God's promise of protection in Psalm 91:12!" Surely, the crowds would hail him as their Messiah King as they would watch him float miraculously and safely to the ground! What a self-serving abuse of the Promises of God!

Again, Jesus responded by asserting the authority of the Written Word of God. *"It is written again, 'You shall not tempt the LORD your God'" (Matthew 4:7).*

The third temptation of Jesus involved *the lust of the eyes.* Satan took Him to a high vantage point with a grand vista revealing the kingdoms of this world in all their splendor. What a glorious sight! Satan then offered it all to Jesus if only He would simply bow down and worship him.

[8]Again, the devil took Him up on an exceedingly high mountain, and showed Him all the kingdoms of the world and their glory. [9]And he said to Him, "All these things I will give You if You will fall down and worship me." (Matthew 4:8-9).

Jesus refused the temptation and, again, quoted God's Word, *"Away with you Satan! For it is written, 'You shall worship the LORD your God and Him only you shall serve'" (Matthew 4:10).*

We cannot love God and hang on to the old way of life. We are to have no other gods before Him (Exodus 20:3). He has no rival. None can compare! He alone is God. He is the all-powerful and benevolent Creator of the Universe, and He demands our unfeigned love and commitment.

After Jesus resisted the devil—again with the Written Word of God—*The devil left Him, and behold, angels came and ministered to Him (Matthew 4:11).* The answer to all the adversities in this life can be solved by realizing that Satan has no choice but to obey the "It is Written!" command. We overcome by the Blood of the Lamb and by the Word of our testimony (Revelation 12:11).

The Reason for the Temptations

Satan's motive for tempting Jesus was to get him to act for Himself, apart from and independent of God. Satan wanted Jesus to disconnect from God, to go His own way, to be His own master, and so to be independent. That is what Satan also wants of us because it leaves us open to his destructive schemes. He wants us to go our own way and neglect our relationship with God. But when we choose to go our own way, we have fallen into Satan's trap.

The Written Word of God is the highest authority to which we can appeal. It carries far greater authority than prophecies, dreams, visions, and audible voices from heaven. Jesus' example certainly makes this clear. When challenged and tempted by Satan, He could have chosen to retaliate by declaring prophecies about Himself, by describing the angelic visitations surrounding His birth, and by recalling the audible voice from heaven: *This is My beloved Son*

(Matthew 3:17). But he didn't counter with these. He used only the Word of God.

Indeed, Jesus knew that the Word of God far superseded all of the prophecies affirming his identity. So, He didn't appeal to the angel Gabriel's visit to his Mother. He didn't appeal to his announcement that the child she would bring forth would be called the *Son of the Highest (Luke 1:32)*. Neither did He appeal to the prophecies of Simeon and Anna (Luke 2:25-38).

> When everything was on the line,
> Jesus went to the highest court of authority
> to which He could appeal:
> The Written Word of God.

When everything was on the line, Jesus went to the highest court of authority to which He could appeal—The Written Word of God. It was by this that Jesus overcame Satan in His humanity, not His deity. He overcame Satan using the same arsenal that is available to each of us who believe. He left a clear, irrefutable example for us to follow.

An Old Testament Revelation of Satan

In his 1919 book entitled *Satan: His Motive and Methods*, renowned Bible teacher and theologian, Lewis Sperry Chafer (1871-1952) wrote the following:

> The world has been willing to comply with the wishes and projects of Satan to the extent of ceasing to believe that he really exists, and this unbelief works advantageously in his present undertakings.

> Yet the opinions of men have never changed the fact of revelation, and, according to the Bible, Satan exists and still possesses great power and influence over the affairs of man—a power and influence to be increasingly dreaded as this present age advances.

Despite modern attempts to dismiss the devil as a myth, the ongoing wars, suffering, and death serve as a reminder that there is an evil being at work in our world. The existence of this evil being and propagator of suffering is clearly spelled out in both the Old and New Testaments. One interesting revelation of his origins is recorded in Ezekiel 28:11-19. This passage describes simultaneously the demise of the King of Tyre and the fall of Lucifer.

> *11Moreover the word of the Lord came to me, saying,*
> *12"Son of man, take up a lamentation for the king of*
> *Tyre, and say to him, 'Thus says the Lord God:*
> *"You were the seal of perfection,*
> *Full of wisdom and perfect in beauty.*
> *13You were in Eden, the garden of God;*
> *Every precious stone was your covering:*
> *The sardius, topaz, and diamond,*
> *beryl, onyx, and jasper, sapphire, turquoise, and emerald*
> *with gold.*
> *The workmanship of your timbrels and pipes*
> *Was prepared for you on the day you were created.*
> *14"You were the anointed cherub who covers;*
> *I established you;*
> *You were on the holy mountain of God;*
> *You walked back and forth in the midst of fiery stones.*
> *15You were perfect in your ways from the day you were*
> *created, till iniquity was found in you.*

16"By the abundance of your trading
You became filled with violence within,
And you sinned;
Therefore I cast you as a profane thing
Out of the mountain of God;
And I destroyed you, O covering cherub,
From the midst of the fiery stones.
17"Your heart was lifted up because of your beauty;
You corrupted your wisdom for the sake of your splendor..." (Ezekiel 28:11-17).

These Scriptures introduce an earthly king, who, with his prideful desire for prominence and dominance, is a perfect picture of Satan. Here are ten things we learn about the devil from this passage.

1. He was embodied perfection (vs. 12).
2. He was full of wisdom (vs. 12).
3. He was very beautiful (vs. 12).
4. He had been in the Garden of Eden (vs. 13).
5. He was dressed in precious stones (vs. 13).
6. He protected the Throne of God (vs. 14-16).
7. He walked amidst precious stones (vs. 14).
8. He was a created being, made by God (vs. 15).
9. He was anointed to off up praise around the Throne of God (vs. 13).
10. Iniquity was found in him because of pride (vs. 17).

Because the devil was puffed up with pride, he lost his exalted place in heaven. He made choices that resulted in his fall. God did not create the devil as a devil. He chose to become God's enemy and consequently, he is doomed to eternity in the lake of fire and brimstone.

> *The devil, who deceived them, was cast into the lake of fire and brimstone where the beast and the false prophet are. And they will be tormented day and night forever and ever (Revelation 20:10).*

Evaluate Everything by The Word

We must remember the example that Jesus left us and check everything with Scripture because God does not work outside of His Written Word. This fact alone should alert us that the stories and popular books about such things as guided tours of heaven or hell, and the like, are not of God. They do not line up with His Written Word.

I am not saying God is limited and cannot work whatever miracle He wishes, but anything and everything He does will line up with His Written Word. Paul confirms the authority of The Word.

> *All Scripture is given by inspiration of God, and is profitable for doctrine, for reproof, for correction, for instruction in righteousness (II Timothy 3:16).*

Television hostess, Oprah Winfrey (b. 1954), has gained notable influence. When she speaks, people listen. So, when she told her audience that a loving God would not consign anyone to everlasting hell, most of her audience applauded. Only a few ladies took issue with her. Of course, she was wrong! But it seems that most people follow her blindly.

In a similar way, it seems that many people in the Church applaud every new trend and novel doctrine. It grieves me to see such ignorance of God's Word. Each of us must take personal responsibility to evaluate what is being taught, regardless of who is doing the teaching.

One example that drives home this truth was the so-called *Laughing Revival* of the 1990s. I am not suggesting that laughter is wrong, but I do believe that the key word is *excessive,* and an honest look at the meetings where this occurred reveal excessive behavior. Such behavior is not confirmed by Scripture, correctly interpreted, and applied.

God's Word is our ultimate guide for all of life, morality, and faith. We are warned never to add to or take away from it.

> *For I testify to everyone who hears the words of the prophecy of this book: If anyone adds to these things, God will add to him the plagues that are written in this book;*
> *19and if anyone takes away from the words of the book of this prophecy, God shall take away his part from the Book of Life, from the holy city, and from the things which are written in this book (Revelation 22:18-19).*

Chapter 9

Repent or Perish

> *From that time Jesus began to preach and to say, "Repent for the kingdom of heaven is at hand."*
> *Matthew 4:17*

When we hear that Jesus was *Very God and Very Man,* most of us struggle to get our mind around that thought. God's thoughts are simply far beyond ours. And this Truth is one that we cannot figure out with our natural minds, nor can we reduce it to human understanding. It is a reality that is revealed only by the Holy Spirit, who is The Teacher.

Yes, Jesus is both truly God and truly human. This was stated by the Council of Constantinople in A. D. 381:

> We believe in one God, the Father, the Almighty, maker of heaven and earth, of all that is seen and unseen. And we believe in one Lord Jesus Christ, the only begotten of the Father, Light from Light, true God from true God, begotten, not made, of one being with the Father . . . For us, humans, and for our salvation, he came down from heaven, was incarnate of the Holy Spirit and the virgin Mary and became fully human. For our sake he was crucified under Pontius Pilate. He suffered death and was buried. He rose again on the third day in accordance

with the Scriptures. He ascended into heaven and is seated at the right hand of the Father. He will come again in glory to judge the living and dead, and his kingdom will have no end.

This is God Incarnate. This is God revealing Himself in human form in the person of Jesus of Nazareth.

1. As a man, Jesus was circumcised on the eighth day according to the Law.
   As God, He fulfilled the Law and redeemed humanity from the curse of the Law by His death and resurrection.
2. As a man, Jesus was baptized in water.
   As God, He baptizes in the Holy Spirit.
3. As a man, Jesus experienced hunger.
   As God, He fed the five thousand.
4. As a man, Jesus wept at the tomb of Lazarus.
   As God, He raised Lazarus from the dead.

IT IS BECAUSE OF WHO HE IS that repentance is a demand with which we must comply. As God, He is the greatest, wisest, and most benevolent being in all the universe. As Our Creator, He is the only person or place where we can find our true purpose and fulfillment.

IN THE LIGHT OF WHO HE IS, how could He not demand absolute repentance and total faith and trust on our part? To allow anything less would only result in our hurt and destruction. No wonder Paul said that he preached *repentance toward God and faith toward our Lord Jesus Christ.*

> [17]*From Miletus he sent to Ephesus and called for the elders of the church.* [18]*And when they had come to him, he said*

to them: "You know, from the first day that I came to Asia, in what manner I always lived among you, [19]serving the Lord with all humility, with many tears and trials which happened to me by the plotting of the Jews; [20]how I kept back nothing that was helpful, but proclaimed it to you, and taught you publicly and from house to house, ***[21]testifying to Jews, and also to Greeks, repentance toward God and faith toward our Lord Jesus Christ*** *(Acts 20:17-21).*

Jesus Teaches Repentance

To repent means "to change the mind." It speaks of a change of purpose, and *Thayer's Greek-English Lexicon* says it refers to "the change of mind of those who have begun to abhor their errors and misdeeds and have determined to enter upon a better course of life."

From the beginning of His public ministry, Jesus made repentance a priority in His Message. *From that time Jesus began to preach and to say, "Repent, for the kingdom of heaven is at hand" (Matthew 4:17).*

Luke records another time when Jesus emphasized the need for repentance. When He heard about how Pilate had butchered some Galilean Jews while they were sacrificing at the Temple in Jerusalem, He used it as an opportunity to show the need for repentance.

[1]There were present at that season some who told Him about the Galileans whose blood Pilate had [a]mingled with their sacrifices. [2]And Jesus answered and said to them, "Do you suppose that these Galileans were worse sinners than all other Galileans, because they suffered

such things? [3]I tell you, no; but unless you repent you will all likewise perish (Luke 13:1-3).

First, He debunked the commonly held notion that bad things always happen to someone because of their sin. Then, He emphasized the need for every one of his listeners to repent. He said, *Do you suppose that these Galileans were worse sinners than all other Galileans because they suffered such things? I tell you, no, but unless you repent you will all likewise perish (vs. 2-3).*

Jesus made it clear that those who refuse to repent have a dreadful eternity awaiting them. He made it clear that it is not enough to have an outward form of religion, but that there must be genuine repentance and faith.

On one occasion, someone asked Him if only a few would be saved. Here's His response!

[23]Then one said to Him, "Lord, are there few who are saved?" And He said to them, [24]"Strive to enter through the narrow gate, for many, I say to you, will seek to enter and will not be able. [25]When once the Master of the house has risen up and shut the door, and you begin to stand outside and knock at the door, saying, 'Lord, Lord, open for us,' and He will answer and say to you, 'I do not know you, where you are from,' [26]then you will begin to say, 'We ate and drank in Your presence, and You taught in our streets.' [27]But He will say, 'I tell you I do not know you, where you are from. Depart from Me, all you workers of iniquity' (Luke 13:23-27).

Prayers for Divine Revelation

It is difficult—No! It is impossible to get our heart and head around such truths unless the Holy Spirit gives us revelation through the Word of God. Something that helped me greatly in this regard was a challenge presented by Dr. Kenneth E. Hagin (1917-2003). He encouraged his audience to pray Paul's Ephesian prayers. The first of these is found in Ephesians 1:17-23, and it is a prayer for both wisdom and revelation concerning the power and blessings that come from Christ's Resurrection. The second is found in Ephesians 3:14-21, and it is a prayer for a revelation of the love of God.

EPHESIANS 1:17-23

17 *That the God of our Lord Jesus Christ, the Father of*
glory, may give to you the spirit of wisdom and
revelation in the knowledge of Him, 18 *the eyes of your*
understanding being enlightened; that you may know
what is the hope of His calling, what are the riches of the
glory of His inheritance in the saints, 19 *and what is the*
exceeding greatness of His power toward us who believe,
according to the working of His mighty power 20 *which*
He worked in Christ when He raised Him from the dead
and seated Him at His right hand in the heavenly places,
21 *far above all principality and power and might and*
dominion, and every name that is named, not only in
this age but also in that which is to come. 22 *And He put*
all things under His feet, and gave Him to be head over
all things to the church, 23 *which is His body, the fullness*
of Him who fills all in all.

EPHESIANS 3:14-21

*[14]For this reason I bow my knees to the Father of our
Lord Jesus Christ, [15]from whom the whole family in
heaven and earth is named, [16]that He would grant you,
according to the riches of His glory, to be strengthened
with might through His Spirit in the inner man, [17]that
Christ may dwell in your hearts through faith; that you,
being rooted and grounded in love, [18]may be able to
comprehend with all the saints what is the width and
length and depth and height—[19]to know the love of
Christ which passes knowledge; that you may be filled
with all the fullness of God. [20]Now to Him who is able
to do exceedingly abundantly above all that we ask or
think, according to the power that works in us, [21]to Him
be glory in the church by Christ Jesus to all generations,
forever and ever. Amen.*

Dr. Hagin challenged us to pray these prayers once a day. I never forgot his words and immediately began to pray those two prayers—not just once a day, but twice a day—once in the morning and once at night.

I want to underline something:
to know the love of Christ which passes knowledge
that you may be filled with all the fullness of God
(Ephesians 3:19b).

My reason for this is to tell you what happened to me. I had been faithfully praying these passages for nine months, when, one night, as I was on my knees praying, these passages seemed to come off the page like a neon light.

It was at that time that revelation knowledge of His Word began to come to me. It was before I began teaching in Bible schools and on satellite. About the same time, one day I was in Dr. Fuchsia Pickett's Bible class, and she was teaching from Ephesians. At one point, I burst into tears and when she asked me why, I could hardly speak. But it was about Ephesians 3:19b! God was confirming that passage again! *To know the love of Christ which passes knowledge that you may be filled with all the fullness of God.*

He was revealing His great love for the world that He had come down from His heaven to save. How can we know the love He feels for us unless by Holy Spirit revelation?

The Healing of a Covenant Woman

I have always been intrigued by Luke's story of Jesus healing the crippled woman (Luke 13). So, I began to pray about why I kept reading it with such interest. Little by little, the light began to shine in my heart about it, revealing things I had never heard preached.

When Jesus called the crippled woman to Him, He knew that she could not straighten her back and that she had been bent over in that incapacitating position for 18 long years. The Holy Spirit opened my understanding to the fact that, throughout those many years, the leaders of the synagogue were also *bent* in the sense that they were uncaring. Think of it! That woman had been coming into the assembly for years, and one wonders if anyone had ever bothered to acknowledge her condition.

But when Jesus saw her, He was immediately moved with

compassion and was sad for her. He called her to Himself and declared, *Woman, you are loosed from your infirmity! (Luke 13:12).* Then, He laid His hands on her and she was immediately made straight and began praising God. The ruler of the synagogue was not happy. In fact, He sharply disapproved, supposedly because Jesus had healed her on the Sabbath. He said to the crowd, *There are six days on which men ought to work; therefore, come and be healed on them and not on the Sabbath day (Luke 13:14).*

Jesus pointed out the hypocrisy and inconsistency of this statement, saying,

> *15Hypocrite! Does not each one of you on the Sabbath loose his ox or donkey from the stall, and lead it away to water it? 16So, ought not this woman, being a daughter of Abraham, whom Satan has bound—think of it—for eighteen years, be loosed from this bond on the Sabbath? (Luke 13:15-16).*

So again, in a sense, the woman's condition paralleled that of the leaders of the synagogue. Their uncaring attitude revealed a bent or twisted attitude! They had a perfect opportunity to repent! But they chose not to turn from religion and not to acknowledge Jesus for Who He was!

This story also reminds us that God does not reject, bend, or torment His own. The woman's condition was the work of the devil. Jesus set her free!

He said that the woman *ought* to be healed because she was a daughter of Abraham. Healing belonged to her because she was a rightful heir of the blessings God promised to him and his descendants (Genesis 12:1-3; 17:1-7).

Now, here is what is exciting! You and I have become partakers of those same blessings through our faith in Jesus Christ. Paul makes this very clear when he says to Gentile believers, *And if you are Christ's, then you are Abraham's seed and heirs according to the promise (Galatians 3:29).*

Christians Are Called to Repent

Jesus loves us just as we are,
but He loves us too, much
to leave us that way.

This is true on a personal level. If we become cold and formal in our faith and lax in our morals, we are to repent. This is also true on a corporate level, as we are the Body of Christ. For example, Jesus strongly rebuked the lukewarm church at Laodicea, and He called them to repent:

> [16]*So then, because you are lukewarm, and neither cold nor hot, I will vomit you out of My mouth. . . .* [19]*As many as I love, I rebuke and chasten. Therefore, be zealous and repent (Revelation 3:16-19).*

Paul, also, called on believers to repent. For example, he reprimanded the Corinthians for several things, including their falling into cliques, their abuse and misuse of Spiritual gifts, and their gross immorality. He warned them about the consequences of their sinful behavior, and he expressed concern that many had not repented.

> [20]*For I fear lest, when I come, I shall not find you such as I wish, and that I shall be found by you such as you do not wish; lest there be contentions, jealousies, outbursts of wrath, selfish ambitions, backbitings, whisperings,*

conceits, tumults; [21]lest, when I come again, my God will humble me among you, and I shall mourn for many who have sinned before and have not repented of the uncleanness, fornication, and lewdness which they have practiced (II Corinthians 12:20-21).

These things are not confined to the Corinthians. It was a real revelation to me when I discovered there was so much sin practiced in the church today and that there was little or no correction. This was highlighted for me when I taught in Bible School in Dallas. We discovered that two of the students were living together but were not married. They refused to accept counsel, claiming that marriage was just a piece of paper. They were dismissed from the school because of their refusal to repent. More than simply dishonoring the rules of the Bible school, they disagreed with God's Word.

Jesus Wept Over Those Who Refused to Repent

God has laid out His will and ways in His Word. So, we are without excuse! And when we refuse His ways, we are setting ourselves up for disaster in this world and for eternal fires in the world to come.

God gets no pleasure out of the death of the wicked. This is one thing that we see when Jesus wept over Jerusalem. As the time of His death approached, He knew that its inhabitants would turn on Him and cry, *"Crucify Him! Crucify Him!"* Yet, His heart was filled with compassion for them, as well as with sadness, because of the devastation that He knew was coming due to their rejection of Him.

[34]O Jerusalem, Jerusalem, the one who kills the prophets and stones those who are sent to her! How often I wanted to gather your children together, as a hen gathers her brood under her wings, but you were not willing! [35]See! Your house is left to you desolate; and assuredly, I say to you, you shall not see Me until the time comes when you say, 'Blessed is He who comes in the name of the LORD (Luke 13:34-35).

That event actually happened when the Romans destroyed the city in 70 A. D.

Persuaded!

In his *Autobiography,* the legendary revivalist Charles G. Finney (1792-1875), who was a converted lawyer, tells of a great revival in Rochester, New York, in which many lawyers and judges were coming to Christ. He tells of a conversation he had with Judge Addison Gardiner, who was a Supreme Court Justice for the State of New York.

The Judge told Finney that he had answered his questions thus far and cleared the way for him to become a Christian. "But," he said, "When you come to the question of the endless punishment of the wicked you will slip up—you will fail to convince us on that question."

When the night came that Finney preached on the eternal punishment of the wicked in hell, he was careful to deal with it as thoroughly as possible. Finney then told what happened when he met Judge Gardiner the next day.

> The next day I met him, and he volunteered the remark at once, "Mr. Finney, I am convinced. Your

dealing with that subject was a success; nothing can be said against it." The manner in which he said this indicated that the subject had not merely convinced his intellect but had deeply impressed him (Garth M. Rosell and Richard A. G. Dupuis, *The Original Memoirs of Charles G. Finney*, 313).

Will You Choose Mercy or Judgement?

> If you reject His infinite love and mercy, then you will experience His infinite justice.

Dear Reader, if you are not a true disciple of Our Lord Jesus, will you repent now? Will you choose today to reject or receive the stupendous LOVE that He has shown to us? If you reject His infinite love and mercy, you will experience His infinite justice.

Repent and Receive Him Now Before It Is Too Late

At the end of every sermon, Dr. Oliver B. Green (1915-1976) would bow his knees and cry, "LORD, SAVE THAT SOUL NEAREST HELL TONIGHT!" Then Jack Holcomb (1921-1968) would sing a song that would bring any sinner to his knees in repentance. One that I remember well is *I Come to the Garden Alone.*

I come to the garden alone
While the dew is still on the roses
And the voice I hear falling on my ear
The Son of God discloses.

Refrain
And He walks with me, and He talks with me,
And He tells me I am His own;
And the joy we share as we tarry there,
None other has ever known.

Verse 2
He speaks, and the sound of His voice,
Is so sweet the birds hush their singing,
And the melody that He gave to me
Within my heart is ringing.

Verse 3
I'd stay in the garden with Him
Though the night around me be falling,
But He bids me go; through the voice of woe
His voice to me is calling.

"I Come to the Garden Alone" was written
by American songwriter C. Austin Miles (1868–1946).

Chapter 10

5 Reasons I Still Believe in Hell

by Dr. Eddie L. Hyatt
www.eddiehyatt.com

> *For God so loved the world that He gave His only begotten Son, that whoever believes in Him should not perish but have everlasting life.*
>
> *John 3:16*

1. Hell is Biblical.
2. Hell is a necessary expression of God's love.
3. Hell is a necessary expression of God's justice.
4. Hell was made necessary by our freedom to choose.
5. Hell has been confirmed by the Holy Spirit.

Recently, I received an email from a person in another state asking my thoughts on hell. She went on to explain that many of her Christian friends have dispensed with the idea of hell and have chided her for being "stuck in religion" for believing in such "an old-fashioned doctrine."

Indeed, many Evangelicals are giving up the doctrine of hell as a place of eternal punishment, arguing that such a belief is not consistent with a God whose chief characteristic is unconditional love. In this essay I will argue, to the contrary, showing that eternal punishment is a necessary expression of God's justice and love, that it is Biblical, that it is necessary because of free-will, and that the Holy Spirit has confirmed this doctrine throughout the history of the Church.

Reason #1
It is Biblical

Jesus talked about hell and warned His hearers to make every effort to avoid the place. Paul and other Biblical writers also warn their readers of the reality of hell as a place of punishment. In the KJV there are two Greek words that are both translated as "hell," *hades* and *ghenna*. The NKJV correctly makes the distinction by translating *hades* as "Hades" and *ghenna* as "hell." Whereas *hades* seems to be the location of the departed spirits of the dead, *ghenna* is the final condemnation and punishment of the unrepentant who persist in their rebellion against God.

Hades, as the place of the departed spirits of those who have died, corresponds to *Sheol* in the Old Testament. It is the word that is used by Jesus in Luke 16:19-31 in the story of the rich man and Lazarus. This story is probably not a mere parable since personal names are attached to the different individuals.

One thing the story teaches is that both the rich man and Lazarus were conscious in the afterlife, one in *Paradise* and the other in torment in *Hades*. Another thing we see is that the rich man could see Abraham and Lazarus in Paradise but could not cross over to them. This, no doubt, added to the rich man's torment.

Hades is also the word used in Matt. 16:18 where Jesus said He would build His church and the gates of *Hades* would not prevail against it. In Revelation 20:14, at the end of the millennium, death and *Hades* are thrown into the lake of fire, probably a reference to *ghenna.*

The *ghenna* (hell) was a garbage dump south of Jerusalem where fires were continually burning. In the New Testament, *ghenna* is used metaphorically of the place of condemnation or punishment in the next life. It is the word used by Jesus in Matthew 5:30 where, to emphasize the horror of final condemnation, He exhorts His hearers that if their right hand causes them to stumble (or sin) to cut it off since it would be better to have only one hand in this life than to have two hands and be thrown into *ghenna.*

This word is also used by Jesus in Matthew 10:28 where He exhorts His listeners to not fear those who kill the body but cannot kill the soul, but to fear Him who has the authority to cast both soul and body into *ghenna. Bauer's Greek-English Lexicon,* the lexicon of choice by students of New Testament Greek, defines *ghenna* as "the place of punishment in the next life."

Some have questioned whether this punishment is eternal by arguing that the Greek word *aionios,* translated "eternal" and "everlasting," actually refers to a long, but finite period of time. While it is true that the noun, *aion,* is sometimes translated "age" in reference to a period of long duration, the adjective, *aionios,* almost always refers to that which is eternal, or without end.

This is borne out by the fact that it is used throughout the New Testament to describe the gift of "eternal" (*aionios*) life to those who believe in Christ. In Romans 16:26 Paul uses it in referring to God Himself as the *everlasting (aionios) God*. The same word is used throughout the New Testament to describe the state of the wicked, *i.e., eternal punishment*.

It is thus used in Matthew 25:46 where Jesus tells of the final judgment where a separation is made of the wicked to His left hand and the righteous to His right. Referring to the final state of both groups, Jesus says, *And these [the wicked] will go away into eternal (aionios) punishment, but the righteous into eternal (aionios) life*.

If *aionios* means "everlasting" in regards to the life that comes from God, then it must carry the same meaning when used of the punishment of the wicked for they are obvious parallel expressions.

Paul uses the same adjective, *aionios,* in II Thessalonians 1:9 where he describes the dire state of the wicked when Christ returns,

> *In flaming fire taking vengeance on those who do know God, and on those who do not obey the gospel of our Lord Jesus Christ. These will be punished with everlasting (aionios) destruction from the presence of the Lord and from the glory of His power.*

Reason #2
Hell Is a Necessary Expression of God's Love

Suppose a serial rapist is released from prison by a liberal judge. He immediately kidnaps an innocent child whom he tortures, rapes, and murders. The rapist is arrested, tried before the same judge, and is found guilty. The judge then sentences him to six months of community service and a $500.00 fine.

Would we say, "Oh, what a loving and kind man is that judge?" No! We would be rightfully outraged because justice, you see, is a necessary component of love. Love without justice is a sugary-sweet niceness that refuses to protect the righteous and do what is right in every situation. Such "love" is worthless and dangerous.

A parent who does not protect his/her children does not love them. Most parents will fight tooth and nail to protect their children, and that is an expression of their love. In a similar way, God will not allow the evil intentions of men and devils to mar the eternal happiness of those who have put their trust in Him. This is why there is a hell.

The modern concept of love that leaves off the element of justice has turned the Sovereign Lord into a heavenly Sugar Daddy who embraces everyone and condemns no one. The inhabitants of heaven, who see more clearly the ghastly ramifications of sin, must be horrified to see the distortion of love in the modern church.

What we are talking about here is the Biblical concept of love that is expressed by the New Testament Greek word *agape*. *Agape* is not flaky or shallow but is just and wise. *Agape* is not a fleeting feeling or emotion but is sensible and rational. It was this *agape* love that brought our Creator down from heaven to offer Himself as a sacrifice for our sins, and the very nature of this love made hell necessary for those who would reject such infinite love.

This is made clear in John 3:16, the love verse of the Bible. It reads, *For God so love the world that He gave His only begotten Son that whoever believes in Him should not* ***perish*** *but have everlasting life.*

This verse says that those who reject this amazing *agape* love and refuse to believe in Jesus Christ, will "perish." The Greek word translated "perish" is *apolumi. Thayer's Greek-English Lexicon* defines this word as meaning "to destroy," "to abolish," and "to devote or give over to eternal misery."

The famed revivalist and converted lawyer, Charles G. Finney, considered hell to be God's eternal prison house where incorrigible rebels against God and his kingdom will be confined and not allowed to spoil the eternal bliss and happiness of those who have accepted the free mercy and grace God has shown to us in Jesus Christ. This is love!

Yes, hell is a necessary expression of God's amazing grace and love.

Reason #3
Hell Is a Necessary Expression of the Justice of God

It is self-evident that a person who commits a crime must be penalized with a punishment that is commensurate with the crime committed. For example, a person with no record who exceeds the speed limit by 5 miles per hour and is sentenced to a year in the county jail and a $5,000.00 fine is not being treated justly.

We would rightfully be outraged at such a travesty of justice. The punishment is not commensurate with the crime committed. We would rightfully suspect that the judge had a malicious bias against the person he sentenced.

That justice is a necessary component of love is confirmed by the stark example mentioned above of a sexual predator who rapes, tortures, and murders an innocent child and then suffers minimal consequences for his crime. Real love will protect the innocent and punish the sinful and wicked.

We should also consider that the guilt is increased when evil is done in return for good. For example, I read a news report of a man in North Carolina who stopped to help the driver of a vehicle who had spun of the road. The man in the ditch was belligerent, struck the man who stopped to help, and then shot him several times, killing him.

What kind of punishment would be appropriate for such horrific evil against a Good Samaritan going out of his way to help? Yet, the just punishment for those who reject the infinite love of God revealed in Jesus Christ must be multiplied many times over.

This is the point Charles Finney made in his preaching on hell and eternal punishment. In his *Autobiography,* he tells of a great revival in Rochester, New York in which many lawyers and judges were coming to Christ. Finney, who was a converted lawyer, tells of a conversation he had with Judge Addison Gardiner, who was a Supreme Court Justice for the State of New York.

The judge told Finney that he had answered his questions thus far and cleared the way for him to become a Christian. "But," he said, "When you come to the question of the endless punishment of the wicked you will slip up—you will fail to convince us on that question."

When the night came that Finney preached on the endless punishment of the wicked in hell, he was careful to deal with it as thoroughly as possible. He showed how those who reject the infinite good of God and His salvation in Christ for their own selfish ends, justly deserve infinite, or endless, punishment.

Finney tells what happened when he met Judge Gardiner the next day. He wrote,

> The next day I met him, and he volunteered the remark at once, "Mr. Finney, I am convinced. Your dealing with that subject was a success; nothing can be said against it" (Garth M. Rosell and Richard A.G. Dupuis, *The Original Memoirs of Charles G. Finney*, 313).

Finney goes on to say, "The manner in which he said this indicated that the subject had not merely convinced his intellect but had deeply impressed him."

In our finite thinking we cannot imagine the magnitude of sin. Sin is not just a finite injustice against a fellow human being; it is a sin against our infinite Creator. Infinite love came down from heaven and provided an infinite sacrifice for our sins. The just punishment for rejecting such infinite love is also infinite, or eternal in nature.

Reason #4
Free Choice Required Hell

I once read a romantic piece in a newspaper about an old

bridge that had been torn down to make way for a new highway. The author ascribed personal virtues to this bridge, speaking of how faithful it had been for so many years, and how it had remained steadfast in the face of wind, rain, snow, cold, and heat.

As I read this, I thought about how there really were no virtues in this bridge, for it was just a heap of metal and concrete. Virtue is found in personhood, and personhood is distinguished by the ability and freedom to think and choose.

Not only is virtue not to be found in inanimate materials such as wood, stone, concrete, and steel, neither is it to be found in feeling. Virtue is ultimately tied, not to our feelings, but to our choices. We are responsible, not for how we feel, but for how we choose.

Love also is tied to the freedom to choose. Where there is no choice, there is no love. Can you imagine being married to a robot—even a very sophisticated one? Anytime you want to hear words of affirmation and love, all you have to do is load the right software and push the right buttons.

We know that would not be satisfying. Love is real because the people involved have chosen to love.

When God created Adam and Eve, He did not create robots or creatures that were programmed to love and serve Him. Creating them in His own image and likeness meant that they would have the ability and the freedom to think, to choose, and to decide if they were going to trust Him and love Him.

In this sense, it was a risky move on God's part to create such beings, for they might choose to rebel against Him. But if there was going to be real love in the relationship, there had to be real freedom to choose.

Yes, God knew beforehand that our first parents would turn from Him. He also knew that countless numbers of their offspring would reject His love and truth. Nonetheless, He considered that the benefits and blessings of creating them outweighed the pain and suffering that He knew would come.

Do you want to know why there is pain and suffering in the world? It cannot be blamed on God. It is because human beings have misused and abused their God-given freedom to choose. Instead of choosing God and His ways, they have chosen to rebel against God and do their own thing, create their own morals, and erect their own standards of truth and righteousness.

It is self-evident that creatures with such freedom to choose, must be held accountable for their choices, and the Bible is clear in this regard. Throughout Scripture there are warnings and exhortations concerning a Day of Judgment.

In Matthew 12:36, for example, Jesus said, *But I say to you for every idle word, they will give account of it in the day of judgment.* And in In II Corinthians 5:10-11, Paul speaks of the judgment of the righteous at the Judgment Seat of Christ. This is not a judgment concerning our worthiness for heaven, but a judgment concerning our motives and how we have lived our lives. Paul says,

For we must all stand before Christ to be judged. We will each receive whatever we deserve for the good or evil we have done in this earthly body. Because we understand our fearful responsibility to the Lord, we work hard to persuade others (NLT).

The great American statesman, Daniel Webster (1782 –1852), when asked what the most sobering thought was to ever enter his mind, replied, "My personal accountability to God."

In Revelation 20:11-12 John describes his vision of the great and final judgment, saying,

> Then I saw a great white throne and Him who sat upon it, from whose face the earth and heaven fled away, And there was found no place for them. And I saw the dead, small and great, standing before God, and books were opened. And another book was opened, which is the Book of Life. And the dead were judged according to their works, by the things which were written in the books.

Yes, mankind's freedom to choose made hell necessary. That is why, in Deuteronomy 30:19, God through Moses urged the people of Israel to make the right decisions and choose life.

I call heaven and earth today as witnesses against you, that I have set before you life and death, blessing and cursing; therefore choose life that both you and your descendants may live.

Reason #5
Hell is Confirmed by the Holy Spirit

There has never been any significant work of the Holy Spirit through the preaching of universalism. I do not know of any example, past or present, in which the preaching of universalism inspired men and women to a greater love for God and a new determination to walk in His truth. On the other hand, preaching on eternal punishment has been a part—even if a small part—of the great revivals of Christian history.

In the First Great Awakening (1730s and 1740s), for example, Jonathan Edward's sermon, *Sinners in the Hands of An Angry God,* captivated the minds and hearts of the masses. The Holy Spirit fell like rain when he read this message from the pulpit. In the Second Great Awakening (1790 – 1840) sermons on hell and Divine retribution were preached along with messages on God's redeeming love and grace. The masses were awakened. Finney's pointed preaching about the Divine justice of eternal punishment turned the hearts and minds of many to Christ and lifted the Church to a new level of commitment and effectiveness. Numerous such examples could be cited from the annals of Christian history and revivalism.

One of the most somber examples comes from the pen of Jonathan Edwards (1703-1758), pastor of the Congregational Church in Northampton, Massachusetts. He was one of the most prominent leaders in the First Great Awakening. He tells of a wicked and intemperate man coming to him one day in a very solemn state of mind. This man related to Edwards an alarming dream he had experienced the previous night. In this dream, he had descended into hell and observed the horrors of that place.

He was told, however, that he was being allowed to return to earth on a one-year probation, the condition being that he must change his manner of life during this time or he would have to return at the end of the year. Edwards was solemnly impressed with the man's dream and assured him that it was a warning from God. Before retiring for the night, Edwards opened his journal and recorded the details of the dream and the date.

Edwards said the man seemed to be serious in his new commitment, leaving off the bottle and faithfully attending church. However, before the year had ended the man returned to his former manner of life. One evening, in a drunken state, he turned to descend a set of stairs when he stumbled and pitched headlong down the stairs breaking his neck and dying instantly.

When Edwards was informed of the tragic news, he opened his journal and somberly noted that that very evening was exactly one year from the time the man had experienced the dream of his one-year probation from hell.

Yes, the Holy Spirit has confirmed the doctrine of hell throughout the history of the church, especially in those Spiritual Awakenings that have revitalized Christendom again and again during times of spiritual malaise and indifference.

These are the reasons I still believe in hell.
Dr. Eddie L. Hyatt (www.eddiehyatt.com)

Chapter 11

How You Can Be Saved

1. Acknowledge that you are a sinner in need of Christ.

   All we like sheep have gone astray; we have turned, every one, to his own way (Isaiah 53:6).

   For all have sinned and fall short of the glory of God (Romans 3:23).

2. Recognize that Jesus Christ provided the sacrifice necessary for your forgiveness and salvation.

   But He was wounded for our transgressions, He was bruised for our iniquities, the chastisement of our peace was upon Him, and by His wounds we are healed (Isaiah 53:5).

   The next day John saw Jesus coming toward him, and said, "Behold! The Lamb of God who takes away the sin of the world" (John 1:29).

3. Repent. This means to turn from your present life to a life that is lived according to God's values as revealed in His Word.

   From that time Jesus began to preach and to say, "Repent, for the kingdom of heaven is at hand" (Matthew 4:17).

... testifying to Jews, and also to Greeks, repentance toward God and faith toward our Lord Jesus Christ (Acts 20:21).

4. Believe in Jesus Christ with all your heart.

   For God so loved the world that He gave His only begotten Son that whoever believes in Him should not perish but have everlasting life (John 3:16).

   And the eunuch said, "See here is water. What hinders me from being baptized?" Then Philip said, "If you believe with all your heart, you may." And he answered, "I believe that Jesus Christ is the Son of God" (Acts 8:36-37).

   If you confess with your mouth the Lord Jesus and believe in your heart that God has raised Him from the dead, you will be saved (Romans 10:9).

5. Pray.

   Almighty God, I ask you to forgive me of my sins. I accept Jesus Christ as my Lord and Savior. I believe He died for our sins and rose again and is seated at the Right Hand of God, and that He will come again to judge all people. In Jesus' Name, Amen!

About the Author

Upon retiring from the faculty of Calvary Cathedral International Bible College in Fort Worth, Texas, Valarie finally had time to research and write this important book that had been on her heart for several years.

She is an ordained minister and renowned Bible teacher. For many years, she taught the uncompromising Word of God throughout the United States, Canada, and in many other nations. She has authored several books and her many Bible courses have been recorded and used in hundreds of Bible schools around the world. Her theme, based on God's Word, has been *Know Your Rights and Stand Your Ground.*

After graduating from North Texas State University, Valarie taught in Texas public schools before being sent forth by God to teach His Word. For several year, she taught in Word of Faith Bible College, and then for 27 years, she was a faculty member at Calvary Cathedral International Bible College. Valarie is an executive member of the Board of Directors of God's Word to Women, Incorporated, and the Int'l Christian Women's Hall of Fame.

Valarie was noted in *The Century of the Holy Spirit,* the premier book reporting on the 20th Century Pentecostal Charismatic Revival, published by Thomas Nelson. The entry is as follows:

> Video and Satellite. The technological revolution that became popular around 1980 opened a whole new way of reaching and teaching, and Word of Faith Bible College (est. 1979) in Dallas, Texas, was

> the pioneer in using this technology. By videotaping the lessons at its home base, the school was able to reproduce them and provide them as a packaged curriculum for local churches who otherwise could not provide high-quality Bible teaching on a regular basis for their hungry constituents. She was the first and only woman to participate as a regular, full-time faculty member in this school, and through what was, at this time, state-of-the-art, cutting-edge technology, she taught thousands of students in hundreds of schools around the globe. When the Bible school switched to live satellite communication in 1983, Valarie was the first and only woman to teach Bible school regularly *via* satellite across America and Canada (p. 260).

Countless lives around the world have been saved and strengthened through Valarie's unwavering obedience to the call of God on her life.

CONTACT INFORMATION

EMAIL:
owenvalarie@yahoo.com

FACEBOOK:
facebook.com/valarie.owen.7

REGULAR MAIL:
Hyatt Int'l Ministries
Attention: Valarie Owen
P. O. Box 3877
Grapevine, TX 76099

Other Books by Valarie Owen

Available from the author and at amazon.com

- In the Beginning God
- Let My People Go!
- Possess the Land
- Wonderful Wisdom
- Christ, Resurrection Life
- Forgiveness: Covenant of Love
- Healing in His Wings
- The Holy Spirit
- Divine Health
- The Blood Covenant
- New Testament Survey Course Manual with Outlines, Readings, and Notes. Written and Compiled by Valarie Owen, Susan Hyatt, and Eddie Hyatt. (This manual is available from Hyatt Int'l Ministries.)

www.ingramcontent.com/pod-product-compliance
Lightning Source LLC
LaVergne TN
LVHW051006080826
845145LV00009B/2485

* 9 7 8 1 8 8 8 4 3 5 5 0 4 *